Benchley
Lost and Found

39 prodigal pieces by

ROBERT BENCHLEY

WITH ILLUSTRATIONS BY
PETER ARNO AND OTHERS

Dover Publications, Inc., New York

Published in Canada by General Publishing Company, Ltd.,
30 Lesmill Road, Don Mills, Toronto, Ontario.
Published in the United Kingdom by Constable
and Company, Ltd.,
10 Orange Street, London WC2.

Benchley Lost and Found is a new collection of 39
humorous essays by Robert Benchley. All of these
articles were originally published in *Liberty* Magazine,
and they are reprinted here by special arrangement
with Liberty Library Corporation.

Standard Book Number: 486-22410-4
Library of Congress Catalog Card Number: 78-88786

Manufactured in the United States of America
Dover Publications, Inc.
180 Varick Street
New York, N.Y. 10014

Contents

"They're Off!"

A Disrespectful View of the Sport of Kings

FOND as I am of horses when meeting them personally (and give me a handful of sugar and I will make friends with any horse—or lose my hand up to the wrist in the attempt) I am strangely unmoved when I see them racing each other up and down a track. A great calm descends on me at the cry "They're off!" and, as the race proceeds, this calm increases in intensity until it is practically a coma, from which I have to be aroused by friends telling me which horse won.

Much of this coolness toward horse racing is due to the fact that I almost never have any money up. I have no scruples in the matter (except that old New England scruple against losing money), but I never seem to be able to get the hang of just how the betting is done. By the time I have decided what horse I would like to bet on, everybody seems to have disappeared, either through indifference to my betting plans or because the race is on. I hear other people betting, but I never can quite see whom they are betting with. The whole thing is more or less chaotic to me.

I am further unexcited through my inability to see the horses after they have started. I have tried using field glasses, but that only makes things worse. I sometimes hold the glasses up to my eyes in an attempt to look sporting, but I find that my arms get tired and the gray film in front of my eyes gets a bit monotonous after several minutes of inspection. The last time I used field glasses at a horse race I thought I saw a rowboat in the distance manned by a suspiciously large number of oarsmen; so I haven't felt like using glasses since then. With my naked eye I can at least see the surrounding country, and without the complication of strange rowboats.

All these distractions to the enjoyment of horse racing I have to contend with in my native land. When, by some slip-up of Fate, I am projected into an English race meeting, my confusion is complete. At American horse races I can see the horses at least start. At English horse races I never can see the horses at all.

This is due, in part, to the prevailing mist (corresponding to our blizzard) which usually settles down over an English course several months before the race and is nicely tucked in at the corners by the day of the big event. In most races they could use camels and no one would know the difference. I once saw a Grand National where forty-three horses left the paddock and disappeared into the fog, after which the spectators hung around and marked cards and told stories for what seemed like about an hour, at the end of which time three horses came out of the fog, one of them having won. Nobody knew what had become of the other forty, and, so far as I know, nobody ever found out. They may be jogging around out there in the mist now. They may never have started. The whole thing might very well have been a frame-up, and all forty-three could quite possibly have just hung around at the barrier until it was time to go in, and tossed up to see which ones went in first. There is no sense in running your head off over a lot of hedges when nobody is going to know the difference. A horse is a fool to tire himself out like that.

Then, too, there are the English race courses. Even if you could see through the fog, you couldn't find them, as they seem to be built on the tunnel system. "Not a horse in sight" is their boast. Watching races in England is more a matter of divination than actual watching. You have to sense where the horses are. I was at the Cheltenham meeting this

spring where the horses evidently started under the grandstand, appeared for a minute in a little gully out in right
field, and then disappeared for good into the beautiful
hills of Gloucestershire. I thought for a while that they were
running away with their riders, as it hardly seemed possible
that people could come all the way from London to watch
a race which was being run in the next county, but pretty
soon they seemed to have been got under control and were
ridden back, through a series of underground passages,
until they finished. As it happened to be a clear day (with
only occasional gusts of snow and rain) you could see the
finish. That is, *you* could. I couldn't, because I was out in a
tent behind the grandstand eating meat pies.

And *there* is a feature of English racing which should not be
overlooked in any enumeration of horrors—the cold meat
pie. It is symbolic of the British holiday. Some one has said
that the English take their pleasures sadly, and I couldn't say
it any better. On a holiday they may be seen walking in
great droves in the pouring rain along an esplanade by the
sea, grim faces buried in raincoat collars, silently giving
themselves over to their mood of merriment with all the
abandon of a file of convicts. Of course, they really haven't
got much to work with in the way of bacchanalia, as most
of England's equipment for merrymaking was captured
from the Boers in 1900 and the dampness reduces confetti
to so many little dabs of cosmetic. But there is also something in the English bulldog spirit which holds out against
any display of hilarity beyond an occasional "pfsho" (this
has to be said through mustaches) or perhaps a muffled
"rippin'." I am not complaining of this as a national trait.
It probably has won England her empire. But, in the mass,
it is a bit depressing. And the cold meat pie is the culinary
symbol of this spirit.

The cold meat pie you will find on exhibition wherever
people are out for a good time. They are usually on a counter of some sort and come in shipments of a dozen, sometimes under a glass cover to keep the crows from swooping
down on them. They look almost like food at first, owing to a

superficial resemblance to a baking-powder biscuit. But on being pressed with a fork, or bitten into, they turn out to be a collection of pastry flakes inclosing a nubbin of meat just large enough to bait a hook for a medium-sized trout. This is to be covered with mustard and devoured greedily, leaving as much of the pastry flakes for the sparrows as you choose. (Several hundred English sparrows got up a petition to keep me in England, so lavish was I with the pastry flakes from my cold meat pies.)

Along with the cold meat pie in the racing buffet goes a sandwich which seems to be made up of those little green strands which collect on a lawn mower on a damp day, but which the sons of the bulldog breed think of as "cress." Now, cress it may be, and water cress at that, but as a man who has fought all his life to keep water cress away from public and private tables because of its unmanly qualities, I may say that the herbaceous material which goes into those English rolls makes an equal amount of water cress seem like one pound of raw meat with a dropped egg on top. One of these and a cold meat pie, and you are as well nourished as a barn swallow. And yet you will see great, red-faced colonels wolfing them down and, what is more, elbowing people out of the way to get at them. Maybe there is a trick about eating them which I didn't catch on to. I must admit that I didn't give the thing my entire attention.

My attention was mostly given over to trying to find the horses, for the race was on and I was all alone. (I always find myself alone at a race, usually having become separated from the rest of my party shortly after entering the inclosure. One of my few excitements at horse racing is seeing how long I can stick with the rest of my party without getting lost.)

I squinted my eyes in the general direction of the course, but by this time the horses were well beyond the intervening hills and meat pies and on their way into Wales. I put my field glasses to my eyes as a desperate last-minute gesture and saw a blue ocean with several old-fashioned derbies floating around in it. This seemed to me to be obviously incorrect; so I took the glasses down again and tried the naked eye. With these I was able to detect three black objects scooting along the horizon, one quite a bit in the lead and the rest bunched.

"Who is that leading?" I asked a gentleman in a raincoat who seemed to be taking an intelligent interest in what was going on. I gathered from his appearance that he was at least one of the Vice Lords of the Admiralty.

Far from giving me an answer to my question, the Vice Lord threw me a dirty look and moved slightly away from me, as if a Board of Health man had just come along and hung a sign on me reading "Scarlet Fever in This House." Asking questions in an American accent is hazardous business in England.

Squinting back again I recovered my three fleeting black objects, but was horrified to see one of them fly straight up into the air, followed almost immediately by the other two. Now, no horse, no matter how well trained, would do that. Certainly not in the middle of a race. A fairly temperamental horse, seeing the race going badly,

If I had been watching the crows all this time, it was pretty discouraging.

might say: "Oh, well, what of it?" and fly up into the air, but he would hardly be followed by the other two.

It was through this line of reasoning that I figured out that the three black objects were not horses. That narrowed it down to crows. If I had been watching three crows all this time, it was pretty discouraging. So I gave the whole thing up and went back into the meat-pie tent.

By this time the place was deserted except for three very unattractive young ladies dressed as nurses who were sweeping up pie flakes.

"Have you any American cigarettes?" I asked, using my best enunciation.

One of the young ladies looked at me and cocked her head inquiringly.

"Do you carry any American cigarettes?" I repeated making a gesture like a cigarette.

The young lady called to some one else who was evidently accustomed to dealing with Germans and Frenchmen.

"American cigarettes?" I shortened the question this time, and did my best to sound like the English actors I have heard in New York. This threw her into a panic, and she summoned a very, very old lady dressed like a very, very old nurse, who came up quite close to me and asked belligerently:

"Qu'est ker say ker voo voolay?"

Suddenly my courage failed me.

"Never mind, I'll smoke my pipe," I said, and rushed from the tent.

I met the crowd who were leaving the course, the race being over. It was the matter of but an hour or two to find one of the members of my party.

"A great race!" I said to him.

"I guess it was," he replied. "I didn't see it."

"You are a madman," I said. "You should stick with me next time."

And I guarantee that any one who sticks with me from now on will see only American horses racing over American courses—and practically none of those.

Sporting Life
in America

Following the Porter

HAVING someone carry your bag for you is a form of sport which has only comparatively recently found favor in America. It has come with the effemination of our race and the vogue of cuffs attached to the shirt.

When I was a boy (and I remember President Franklin Pierce saying, "What a boy!" too) to let a porter carry your bag was practically the same as saying: "My next imitation will be of Miss Jenny Lind, the Swedish Nightingale." No man who could whistle or chin himself would think of it. In the days before these newfangled steam cars started raising Old Ned with our apple orchards with their showers of sparks, I have seen men knock a porter down for even reaching for their valises. The only people who would consider such a thing were veterans of the Mexican War who had lost both arms above the elbow or traveling salesmen for pipe-organ concerns. The traveling salesmen could let a porter take one end of the pipe organ without incurring the sneers of their fellow travelers.

But nowadays it is a pretty unattractive porter who can't wheedle a great hulking man out of his brief case, even if he is just crossing a platform to take another train. And I am secretly glad of this change in the standards of virility; for, frankly, my arms used to get awfully tired in the old days. This was due, in part, to the fact that any suitcase I ever buy always weighs a minimum of sixty pounds without anything in it. It is something about belonging to *me* that makes a suitcase put on weight. I lift other people's suitcases and they are like thistledown. But mine, with perhaps two collars and a tube of shaving cream in it, immediately swells up and behaves like the corner stone of a twenty-story building. I know that this is not just my imagination, because several people have tried to steal my suitcase and have complained to me about its being so heavy.

But even now I still have a slightly guilty feeling as I walk up the runway with a porter going on ahead with my bags. I try to look as if I were not with him, or as if he had snatched up my luggage by mistake and I were trying to catch him to take it myself. If it is very obvious that he is with me, I carry my right arm as if I had just hurt it badly. You can't blame a cripple for not carrying his own bag.

It is not only the impression that I must be making on other people that worries me. I feel a little guilty about the porter. If the bag is very heavy (as it always is, and not from what you think, either) I start out with a slightly incoherent apology to him, like: "You'll find that pretty heavy, I'm afraid," or "Don't do this if you don't really feel like it." Sometimes I tell him what I have in the bag, so that he will understand. "Books," I say, timidly. (He never believes this.) I have even been so specific, if the thing was very heavy, as to tell him that I was carrying home a law digest and a copy of the Home Book of Verse for a friend. If this doesn't seem to be making him feel any better, I add, "—and shoe-trees. They make a bag heavy." Several times I have worked myself up into such a state of sympathy for the man that I have taken one handle of the bag myself. There is one bag in particular that worries me. It is what the French refer to as a *grand valise* and I don't know what I was thinking of when I bought it. Standing on a station platform it looks like a small rhinoceros crouching for a spring, and I have seen porters run ten feet to one side of it rather than be called upon to lift it.

It holds a great deal more than I have got to put into it, including two small boys, but even with my modest equipment it has to be lifted on and off boats with a crane. There is a story about Louis XVI having hidden his horse in it during the early days of the Revolution, but I rather doubt that, as there would have been no place for the horse to breathe through. However, the fact remains that I don't know what I was thinking of.

Now, this bag is all right when I am abroad, for the porters over there are accustomed to carrying anything up to and including a medium-size garage. They hitch it to a strap with another load the same size on the other end, fling it over their shoulders, perspire freely, and trot off. I would be very glad to feel sorry for them, but they don't seem to mind it at all. It is an older civilization, I guess.

But in the United States I am very uneasy about this bag. I apologize to the porter who puts it on the train and feel that I have to give him enough extra to endow a Negro college in his home town. I start worrying about getting it into a taxi long before the train has pulled into the station, and I run over in my mind a few pleasantries with which I can assuage the porter on the other end. "Pretty heavy, eh? And I don't drink, either! Aha-ha-ha-ha!" or "Maybe I'd better get a trunk, eh?" None of these ever go very big, I may add.

It usually ends up by my being so self-conscious about the thing that I carry it myself. There are two ways of doing this: one is to carry it by the handles, but that way it crashes heavily against the side of the leg and eventually throws me; the other method is to hoist it up on the shoulder and stagger along under it. This is not much better, for then it not only cocks my hat over my eye but completely shuts off my vision from the other eye, so that many times I have walked head on into another train or collided with passengers. I have even caught up with passengers going in the same direction and smashed into them from behind. And the combined weight of my body and the bag, going at a fair clip, is sufficient to capsize and badly bruise a woman or a small man.

Taxi drivers are not very nice about my bag, either.

When confronted with the problem of where to put it in the cab, they often make remarks such as: "Why don't we put the cab on top of the bag and drag it through the streets?" or "Where are the elephants?" With my bag tucked on the front seat beside him, a taxi driver has to lean out over the other side and drive with one knee. And nobody feels sadder about it than I do. Of all people to have a bag like that, I am the worst, because I am so sensitive.

It is not only with railway porters that I am ill at ease. I feel very guilty about asking moving men to carry bureaus and bookcases downstairs. I have a bookcase which I sold to a man three years ago which is still standing in my room because I could not get up courage to ask anyone to move it for me. I know that there are men who make it their business to lift heavy articles of furniture, but this is a *terribly* heavy bookcase. The first six weeks after I sold it I used to sit and look at it and say to myself: "I really ought to get that over to Thurston right away." But I couldn't seem to feel right about getting anyone to do it.

I tried hitching it along the floor myself, but I couldn't even get it away from the spot where it had always been. So then I tried forgetting about it, and would look quickly away every time my eyes rested on it. Thurston asked me about it once, and I said that I had been trying to get a moving man to take it but that there was a strike on. I tried draping it with a sheet, so that I wouldn't have to look at it, but that did no good. The sheet just made it worse.

About a year ago I gave Thurston his money back and said that I had decided to keep the bookcase, but I really don't want it. Perhaps some moving man will see this confession and will come up some day and ask me if I don't want some especially heavy furniture moved. If he *asked* me, I couldn't feel guilty about it, could I? But I can tell him right now that it is heavier than he thinks, and I won't blame him if he drops it on the stairs, and I would rather not watch, if he doesn't mind.

It makes it very difficult to be afraid to impose on porters and yet not to be able to carry things yourself. Perhaps the best thing to do would be just not to own any heavy things, and to buy whatever clothes and shoes I need in the town I happen to be in. Or perhaps it would be better yet not to go anywhere, and just sit in my room.

The Return of
the Bicycle

A Conservative Huzza

WITH the complete collapse of the automobile as a means of transportation (I believe that I am correct in assuming that it has been a miserable fiasco and will soon be seen on our roads only in the form of heavy trucking vehicles or agricultural tanks), and with the failure to leave the ground of practically every airplane constructed in the last six months, thereby eliminating aviation as a factor in future travel, there remains but one solution to the problem of those of us who want to get from one place to another. We must go back to the bicycle.

We were fools ever to leave the bicycle. I remember being quoted at the time in Handlebar and Sprocket, the great bicycle journal of the day, as saying: "Mark my words, you horseless-carriage fiends and flying-machine bugs! The day will come when you will forsake your senseless toys, which have not even the sanction of natural laws, and will come crawling back to the safety bicycle, begging to be given a ride, even on the handlebars."

Well, the day has come, and it is going to cost those people anywhere from fifty to seventy-five cents apiece if they want to ride on *my* handlebars. A dollar if they want to ring the bell themselves.

It was obvious from the start that the automobile and airplane were impractical. Any agencies of propulsion which depend upon such tricky outside helps as gasoline, heavy motors, slip covers, and radiator caps are, on the face of it, no good for general use. And as for being dependent on wind and weather, the old-fashioned sailing ship was discarded because of that very drawback. The bicycle calls for nothing in the way of accessories except a pair of sturdy calves and a wire basket to carry lunch in. Gas? No, sir, thank you! Fog? Ha-ha! Spark plugs? Head winds? Indeed! It was hop on and away and the devil take the hindmost! It will seem good to have those days back again.

Of course, there will be some die-hards who will insist for a while on pushing their old automobiles out on the roadway and blocking traffic with them. Such reactionaries must be dealt with summarily. The new code of traffic regulations should make it obligatory for those who wish to chug along in motor vehicles to keep close to the right-hand side of the road and to draw over into the gutter whenever a bicycle club riding five or more abreast wishes to pass. (Bicycle clubs have already begun springing up all over the country, reviving their old charters and buying new blazers.)

All motors giving off a carbon-monoxide exhaust or in any other way interfering with the vision or comfort of cyclists who happen to be behind them should be confiscated and the owner obliged to wheel his chassis home across the fields.

Any parking of motor vehicles which makes it impossible for cyclists to draw up to the curb should be done away with. If motorists want to leave their "cars" anywhere, let them leave them at home where they will be out of decent people's way. A set of rules along these lines would soon do away with what few automobiles may survive the debacle which is already drawing near.

I feel a more or less personal interest in this revolt against motor and air transportation because I have reason to believe that it is an ancestor of mine who is depicted in the oldest existing record of the cult of self-propulsion. In a stained-glass window in a church at Stoke Poges, Buckinghamshire, England, is shown the figure of a man astride a wheeled instrument, which students of bicycle

"And if you fall, you have farther to fall and just that much more fun and excitement."

pictures claim to be the earliest attempt by any artist to show self-cycling.

This man is apparently propelling himself by pressing his feet against the ground with a forward pushing movement, using the wheel more or less to lean against, with probably a little high-spirited coasting now and then. I have seen the window, and the man looks quite a lot like me, except for a full beard and a more nervous expression around the eyes. The name underneath the figure is in Gothic letters and very difficult to make out, but it certainly begins with a "Ben" and the rest seems to be something of a compromise between "wgaalle" and "chhaalle."

Now, my people originally came from Wales (which, in itself, would account for the spelling), and, for a man with a contraption like the one in the picture, a spin from Wales to Buckinghamshire would have been mere child's play. As I figure it out, this man Benwgaalle or Benchhaalle built his bicycle, took along some lunch, and pushed himself along to Stoke Poges, at which place he became a sort of local hero, like Lindbergh at Le Bourget, and a stained-glass window was made in his honor. I rather imagine that he stayed in Stoke Poges all the rest of his life, as he probably was pretty lame.

Having seen this evidence of the pioneering activities of my ancestor in self-propulsion, I took the trouble to look up the records and see who followed his lead. There is a record in 1818 of a man named Denis Johnson of Long Acre making an improvement on the original Benchley model, but the market price of the machine was so high that very few could afford it, and it became scornfully known as the "dandy horse." Pushing the feet against the ground was still the method of obtaining power, so the dandies of that day must have been a great deal more agile than dandy. In fact, at the end of a ride in the country it must have been hard to tell them from anyone else.

It was not until 1840 that the first real bicycle was constructed by Kirkpatrick McMillan of Dumfries, Scotland, who was immediately arrested for "furious driving on the roads." This put an end to any further improvements from Kirkpatrick. He probably got sulky after that and never left his house. But his soul went scorching on and the bicycle became a reality, with what was considered the last word in bicycle building in 1873.

It is not difficult to imagine the selling talk of the first agent for this model: "I'll tell you, Mr. Waterous. The trouble with the bicycle up to now has been that both wheels have been of the same size. Now, our 1873 model has a very radical departure in body building. The front wheel is *twice* the size of the back wheel, thereby eliminating all the jarring and bouncing of the other makes. You are also up a great deal higher and can see more of the surrounding country as you ride. And if you fall, you have farther to fall and just that much more fun and excitement.

"I need hardly tell you, Mr. Waterous, that the cyclist who buys one of our models right now, before the price goes up, will never regret it and will be the most envied man in his neighborhood."

If he is alive today there probably is no more bitter person in the world than the inventor of the high-wheeled bicycle. He is probably still claiming that he was "crowded out" by the combine in 1885 when the high wheel was abolished and the "safety" introduced.

But it is the "safety" bicycle which has come to stay, and which is now about to sweep the flash-in-the-pan automobile from the roads and the unreliable airplane from the skies. The bicycle has been lying low all these years while the Wright brothers and Ford have been experimenting. We old cyclists have been keeping quiet and letting the fly-by-night innovations run their course. And now that our predictions are coming true, we are donning our trouser clips and pulling our caps over our eyes, crouched over our handlebars in silent expectation. At the word "Go!" we will sweep down the road, and it needs must be a nervy automobilist who will stand in our way.

The only trouble is that I can't find my bicycle.

Ding-Dong School Bells

Or What the Boy Will Need

ALTHOUGH it hardly seems credible, it is almost time to begin packing the kiddies off to school again. Here they have been all summer, the rascals, tracking sand into the dining room, rolling Grandma about, and bringing in little playmates who have been exposed to mumps (when Daddy himself hasn't had mumps yet, and mumps for Daddy would be no fun), and in all kinds of ways cheering up the Old Manse to the point of bursting it asunder.

And now the school bells will be ringing again! A sure sign of the coming outbreak of education is the circulars which come in the mail from the clothing and general outfitting stores with lists of "required articles for the schoolboy and for the schoolgirl," just as if the schoolboy and the schoolgirl couldn't tell you themselves exactly what they are going to need—and more, too. Some day I want to get one of those list-compilers to come round and listen to my son and my daughter make out *their* lists. They will have him crying his heart out with chagrin inside of three minutes. "One rubber slicker," indeed! "One green slicker, one tan slicker, one old-rose slicker," is more like it. That is in case the rain comes in three different colors.

I can remember the time (by pressing my temples very hard and holding my breath) when the opening of school meant simply buying a slate with a sponge tied to it and a box of colored crayons. No one, to my knowledge, ever used a slate and a sponge. They were simply a sentimental survival of an even earlier day which the man in the stationery store forced on children who were going to school. The colored crayons were, of course, for eating.

But we bought our slates and our sponges and our crayons (sometimes with a ruler for slapping purposes), and then never used them, for the school furnished all the pencils and pads of yellow paper which were necessary. One of the great releases of my grown-up life has been that I don't have to write on a yellow sheet of paper with blue lines ruled on it half an inch apart. I don't *like* to have to write my lines half an inch apart, and now that I am a great big man, I don't do it. That is one of the advantages of graduating from school.

Today, however, although the slate and the sponge have been removed from the list, there are plenty of "incidentals" even for those children who go to what are known as public schools. What with the increase in high-school fraternities and fixings, high school today resembles the boarding school of yesterday, the boarding school of today resembles the college of yesterday, and the college of today (let's see if I can keep this up) has turned the corner and resembles the public school of yesterday. Is that clear? Or shall we go over it just once again?

Of course, according to the clothing-store lists, once your child gets into a so-called private school (which means that no child who has killed an uncle, an aunt, or any nearer relative, can enter) he is in for an outfitting such as hasn't been seen since Byrd started for the South Pole. You wouldn't think that merely sleeping away from home, in a nation as strict as ours, would entail so many extra clothes for a child.

And not night clothes, either. A boy, when he is living at home, may just sit around the house reading and grousing all day, but the minute he gets away at school (according to the lists) he goes in for fox-hunting, elk-hunting, and whatever it is they hunt with falcons (Falcon hood, $45.50). Then for caber-tossing, you can get a good caber for $24, but the suit that you have to wear must be made by a Scottish tailor out of regulation St. Andrews heather, made up into a smart model for $115.

As I remember my school requirements (I am both a public and a private school boy myself, having always changed schools just as the class in English in the new school was taking up Silas Marner, with the result that it was the only book in the English language that I knew until I was eighteen—but, boy, did I know Silas Marner!), I would substitute a list something like the following in place of that sent out by the clothing store:

One sheet of note paper (with envelope to match) for letter home. This should do for the school year. Requests for money can be made by telegraph, collect.

Five hundred pairs of socks, one to be thrown away each day.

One hat, in a hatbox, the key of which will be left with

One hat in a hatbox. Five hundred pairs of socks. One overcoat. One old model Ford.

the school principal for safekeeping until the end of the term.

One overcoat, to be left with the hatbox key, *unless* the overcoat is of raccoonskin, in which case it should be made adaptable for wear up to and including June 10.

One copy, in clear English translation, of each of the following books: The Æneid, Odyssey, Immensée, La Fontaine's Fables (be sure that this follows the original French; there are a lot of fancy English adaptations which will get you into trouble with words which aren't in the text), Nathan the Wise, and Don Quixote. There should be plenty of room between the lines in these books, to allow for the penciling in of a word now and then.

One rubber mouth appliance, for making the sound commonly known as "the bird."

One old model Ford, with space for comments in white paint.

One pipe, with perhaps an ounce of tobacco, for use about four times, then to be discarded or lost.

One pocket lighter, made to harmonize with the other bureau ornaments.

Three dozen shirts, with collars already frayed to save the laundry's time.

One very old T-shirt.

Three dozen neckties, for use of roommates.

One set of name tags, to be sewn on clothing to insure roommate's getting them in return for clothing marked with roommate's name.

There is no sense in trying to provide handkerchiefs.

Here, then, Mr. Boy's Outfitter, is my list. I think that it takes care of everything. I am not prepared to go into as much detail as to the requirements for a girl's school, because my daughter (if I had one) is not old enough. But I don't want to get any more intimations that I am not doing right by my boy if I don't buy him a red hunting coat. If he wants a red hunting coat, he can let the sleeves of mine down an inch or so and wear that.

$S$and Trouble

It doesn't seem much more than a month since I shook the remaining grains of last season's sand out of my shoes. Here's another summer nearly gone, and I find I am doing it again.

By "It" I mean the process of getting sand on and into things and then getting it off and out of things, at which most of us spend our summers. If, during the winter months when we are in the city, we had to cope with an element as cussed as sand, we would be writing letters to the papers and getting up committees to go to the City Hall about it. If, every night when we got home from work, we had to shake out our shoes and empty out our pockets to get rid of a fine scratchy substance which was infesting the city, there would be such a muttering all over town that you would think there was a thunderstorm coming up. And yet, when it is a part of our vacation, we take it, along with all other inconveniences, and pay money for it. It sometimes seems as if we weren't very bright.

Of course, there is sand and sand. I am a great admirer of nice, hard, smooth sand which knows its place, especially if I can draw pictures in it with a stick. I guess there is no more exquisite pleasure. It is a little more enjoyable if you happen to be able to draw well, but even just little five-pointed stars and egg-and-dart designs are a great comfort. Sand is also a good place on which to write, "I love you," as it would be difficult to get it into court after several years have passed.

But a great majority of the grains of sand on the earth's surface do not know their place. They are always wanting to go somewhere—with you. Just how several hundred grains of sand work it to get up from the beach and into the short hair on the back of your neck is one of Old Mother Nature's mysteries, but they do it, and with a great deal of dispatch, too. I can go on to a beach and stand perfectly upright, touching nothing but the soles of my feet to the ground, for four minutes, with my hands held high above my head, and at the end of that time there will be sand in my pockets, on the back of my neck, around my belt line (inside), and in my pipe. It is marvelous.

Smoking is one of life's pleasures which is easiest marred by this little trick of sand. After a swim in the ocean or lake there is nothing more refreshing than the tang of tobacco smoke, yet the risks incident to lighting a pipe or a cigarette are so great that it is hardly worth while. A pipe is particularly susceptible. You can wait until you have had your swim and then have a man come down from the bathhouse with a fresh pipe in a chamois bag, which he himself can insert in your mouth (naturally, not still in the chamois bag) and which he can light for you with matches also brought freshly to the beach, handled only with silk gloves. And yet, at the first drag, there will come that sickening crackling sound like an egg frying in deep fat, indicating that the stem is already as full of sand particles as a shad is of roe, and presently your teeth are a-grit (and on your teeth three grains of sand will do the work of thousands) and in no time sand is in your eye.

Just to avoid this blight on beach smoking I had a leather-smith make me a little box, with compartments just fitting my pipe, a box of cigarettes, a box of matches, and my watch. (Sand in watches would make a whole treatise in itself.) Although I came under suspicion of carrying a vanity case when I appeared on the beach with this outfit, it nevertheless seemed worth it to keep my smoking utensils free from the usual pulverized rock. But the very first day, when I came out of the water and, unwrapping my box from two towels, unlocked it with a combination known only to myself and my banker, I found that my pipe, cigarettes, and matches were merely parts of a sand design such as men build along by the boardwalk at Atlantic City. In fact, there was more sand on them than usual, because the box had served as a catchall in which sand could concentrate and pile up without being blown away by the breeze. Since then I have given up smoking on the beach.

Lying supine (or even prone, for that matter) on the sand is one of those activities which always seem more fun just before you do them. You think how wonderful it would be to stretch out under the sun and bake, letting the world, as the Duncan Sisters used to do in soprano and alto, go drifting by. So you take up your favorite position (which very shortly turns out to be *not* your favorite position, much to your surprise) and, shutting your eyes, abandon yourself to a pagan submission to the sun and its health-giving beams.

Gradually small protuberances arise from the beach underneath you, protuberances which were not there when you lay down but which seem to have forced their way up through the sand for the express purpose of irritating you. If you are lying on your face, the sand just at the corner of your mouth raises itself up in a little mound just high enough to enter between the upper and lower lip. If you are lying on your back, the same sand raises itself into an even higher mound and one with a curve at the top so that it still gets into the corner of your mouth. All this happens without outside aid.

But there is plenty of outside aid available. One small boy playing tag fifty feet away, and running past anywhere within that radius, can throw off enough sand to blind an ordinary man. And, as there must be at least two small boys to make a game of tag anything but a mockery, enough sand is thrown off to blind two ordinary men. A dog, merely by trotting by, can get almost the same effect. And it is very

One small boy can throw enough sand to blind an ordinary man.

seldom that a dog is content with merely trotting by. I have never yet stretched myself on a beach for an afternoon's nap that a dog, fresh from a swim, did not take up a position just to the left of my tightly closed eyes, and shake himself. I need hardly go into this.

Aside from the initial fright at the sudden shower, there is the subsequent irritation at the humiliation (it is quite apparent that the dog picked you out deliberately to do it to) which ends in your leaping up and going home to lie down on a couch. It usually ends up that way even without the dog.

I am perhaps working myself up into a phobia for sand which I did not originally feel. Simply by putting all this down on paper I have got myself to itching down the back of my neck and find myself wiping my lips to get off imaginary particles of sand. And there is no sense in my getting myself into this state of nervous susceptibility, for in fifteen minutes I have got to go down to the beach and romp with the children. Perhaps I can persuade them to go to the movies. Perhaps I shall even *make* them go to the movies.

*T*he *T*ruth about *T*hunderstorms

ONE of the advantages of growing older and putting on
weight is that a man can admit to being afraid of certain
things which, as a stripling, he had to face without blanching.
I will come right out and say that I mean thunderstorms.

For years I have been concealing my nervousness during
thunderstorms, or, at least, I have flattered myself that
I was concealing it. I have scoffed at women who gave signs
of being petrified, saying, "Come, come! What is there
to be afraid of?" And all the time I *knew* what there was
to be afraid of, and that it was a good, crashing sock on
the head with a bolt of lightning. People *do* get it, and
I have no particular reason for believing that I am immune.
On the contrary.

Just where any of us in the human race get off to adopt
the Big-Man attitude of "What is there to be afraid of?"
toward lightning is more than I can figure out. You would
think that we knew what lightning is. You would think
that we knew how to stop it. You would think that no one
but women and yellow dogs were ever hit by it and that
no man in a turtle-neck sweater and a three days' beard
on his chin would give it a second thought. I am sick of all
this bravado about lightning and am definitely abandoning
it herewith.

Ever since I was a child old enough to have any pride
in the matter I have been wincing inwardly whenever

100,000 volts of Simon-pure electricity cut loose in the air. My nervous system has about six hundred ingrowing winces stored up inside it, and that is bad for any nervous system. From now on I am going to humor mine and give a shrill scream whenever I feel like it, and that will be whenever there is a good sharp flash of lightning. I will say this for myself: I will scream when the lightning flashes and not when the thunder sounds. I may be timid but I am no fool.

My nervousness begins when I see the black clouds in the distance. At the sound of the first rumble my digestive system lays off work, leaving whatever odds and ends of assimilation there may be until later in the day.

Of course, up until now I have never allowed myself to show trepidation. If I happened to be out on the water or playing tennis when it was evident that a storm was coming, I have looked casually at my watch and said, "Ho-hum! What about going in and making a nice, cool drink?" Sometimes I even come right out and say, "It looks like a storm—we'd better get in"; but there is always some phlegmatic guy who says, "Oh, we aren't going to get that—it's going around the mountain," and, by the time it is evident that we *are* going to get that and it *isn't* going around the mountain, it is too late.

It is remarkable how slow some people can be in taking down a tennis net or bringing a boat inshore when there is a thunderstorm on the way. They must not only take the net down but they must fold it up, very carefully and neatly, or they must put things away all shipshape in the cabin and coil ropes. Anything to waste time.

My attempts to saunter toward the house on such occasions must have, at times, given away the dread I have of being the recipient of a bolt of lightning. I guess that I have done some of the fastest sauntering ever pulled off on a dry track. Especially if my arms are loaded down with cushions and beach umbrellas I make a rather ungainly job of trying to walk as if I didn't care and yet make good time.

If possible, I usually suggest that someone run ahead and shut the windows in the house, and then immediately delegate myself to this job. I am not so crazy about shutting windows during a thunderstorm, but it is better than hanging around outside.

I once got caught up in an airplane during an electrical storm. In fact, there were *two* storms, one on the right and one on the left, and we were heading right for the spot where they were coming together. We could see them quite a long time before they hit us, and I was full of good suggestions which the pilot didn't take. I wanted to put down right where we were. It was a rocky country, covered with scrub pines, but it seemed to be preferable to hanging around up in the air.

I was considerably reassured, however, by being told (or shouted to) that you are safer up in the air during a

If my arms are loaded down I make a rather ungainly job of trying to walk as if I didn't care and yet make good time.

thunderstorm than you are on the earth, as lightning cannot
strike unless the object is "grounded." It sounded logical
to me, or as logical as anything connected with lightning
ever could sound, and I sat back to enjoy my first electrical
display in comfort. It really was great, although I hate to
admit it. You couldn't hear the thunder because of the
motors and there were some very pretty flashes.

It was only several months after, on reading of a plane
being struck by lightning three thousand feet up, that I
began to get nervous. Perhaps you can't get hit unless you
are "grounded," according to all the laws of nature, but it
is always the exception that proves the rule, and it would be
just my luck to be one of the exceptions.

Perhaps the worst part that a nervous man has to play
during a crisis like this is reassuring the ladies. If I am alone,
I can give in and go down cellar, but when there are women
around I have to be brave and joke and yell "Bang!"
every time there is a crash. To make matters worse, I find
that there are a great many women who are not frightened,
and who want to sit out on the porch and play bridge
through the whole thing.

This is a pretty tough spot for a man of my temperament.
At best, I am an indifferent bridge player, even with the
sun shining or a balmy summer night's breeze wafting
around outside. I have to go very carefully with my bidding
and listen to everything that is being said or I am in danger
of getting a knife in my back from my partner when the game
is over. But with a thunderstorm raging around my ears and
trees crashing down in the yard by my elbow, I might just
as well be playing "slapjack" for all the sense I make.

A good flash of lightning has been known to jolt a "Five
spades" out of me, with an eight and queen of spades in my
hand. Sometimes it would almost have been better if the
bolt had hit me. (Only fooling, Lord! Just kidding!)

I would feel more ashamed of confessing all this if I
weren't sure that I am in the right about it. I am not afraid
of snakes or burglars or ghosts or even Mussolini, but when
it comes to lightning—boy, there's something to be afraid *of!*

And anyone who says that he isn't is either lying or an awful sap.

Of course, being nervous isn't going to keep you from getting hit, but when you are nervous you don't lie around with water dripping on you and holding a copper plate in your mouth, and avoiding all this sort of thing certainly helps.

If I were running a thunderstorm I would pick out some big man who goes around saying there is nothing to be afraid of and clip a cigar or two out from between his teeth just to show him. And any nice guy like me, who knows his place and tries to keep it, I would let go scot-free and might even uproot a fine big pot of buried gold pieces for him.

The funny part about all this is that now that I am old enough to come out frankly and admit how I feel about thunderstorms, I seem to be getting too old to mind them so much. It has been a couple of years now since I had a really good scare (I am now knocking wood so hard that the man in the next room just yelled "Come in!"). Perhaps it is just that, when you get to be my age, it doesn't make so much difference. If it isn't lightning, it will be hardening of the arteries. I still would prefer hardening of the arteries, however.

"*A*bandon *S*hip!"

THERE has been a great deal of printed matter issued, both in humorous and instructive vein, about ocean travel on those mammoth ships which someone, who had never ridden on one, once designated as "ocean greyhounds." "Ocean camels" would be an epithet I would work up for them, if anyone should care enough to ask me. Or I might even think of a funnier one. There is room for a funnier one.

But, whether one calls them "ocean greyhounds" or "ocean camels" or something to be thought up at a later date, no one can deny that the ships which ply between this country and foreign lands get all the publicity. Every day, throughout this "broad" land of ours, on lakes, rivers, gulfs, and up and down the coast line, there are plying little steamers carrying more American passengers than Europe, in its most avid moments, ever dreamed of. And yet, does anyone ever write any travel hints for them, other than to put up signs reading: "Please leave your stateroom keys in the door on departure"? Are colorful sea stories ever concocted, or gay pamphlets issued, to lend an air of adventure to this most popular form of travel by water? I hope not, for I had rather hoped to blaze a literary trail in this tantalizing bit of marine lore.

There are three different types of boat in use on our inland waterways and coastwise service: (1) Ferries, which are so silly that even *we* won't take them up for discussion.

(2) Day, or excursion, boats, which take you where you are going, and, if you get fascinated by the thing, back in the same day. (3) Night boats, mostly in the Great Lakes or coastwise service, which have, as yet, never fascinated anyone to the point of making a return trip on the same run. And then, of course, you can always row yourself.

There is one peculiar feature of travel on these smaller craft of our merchant marine. Passengers are always in a great hurry to embark and in an equally great hurry to disembark. The sailing of an ocean liner, on which people are really going somewhere and at considerable expense, is marked by leisurely and sometimes haphazard arrivals right up to the last minute. But let an excursion boat called the Alfred W. Parmenter announce that it will leave one end of a lake at 9 A.M. bound for the other end of the lake and return, and at 6 A.M. there will be a crowd of waiting passengers on the dock so great as to give passers-by the impression that a man-eating shark has just been hauled up. On the other hand, fully half an hour before one of these "pleasure" boats is due to dock on its return trip, the quarter-deck will be jammed with passengers who evidently can hardly wait to get off and who have to be restrained by the officers from jumping overboard and beating the boat in to shore. At least a quarter of the time on one of these recreation trips is spent in standing patiently in a crowd waiting for a chance to be the first ones on and the first ones off.

Just why anyone should want to be the first one aboard an excursion boat is one of the great mysteries of the sea. Of course, there is the desire to get good positions on deck, but even if you happen to be the first one on board, the good positions are always taken by people who seem to have swum around and come up from the other side. And then there is the question: "What *is* a good position?" No matter where you settle yourself, whether up in the bow or 'way aft under the awning, by the time the boat has started it turns out to be too sunny or too windy or too much under the pattering soot from the stack. The first fifteen minutes of a trip are given over to a general changing of positions among the passengers. People who have torn on board and fought for preferred spots with their lives are heard calling out: "Here, Alice, it's better over here!" and "You hold these and I'll go and see if we can't get something out of the wind." The wise tripper gets on board at the last minute and waits until the boat has swung around into her course. Then he can see how the sun, wind, and soot are falling and choose accordingly.

Of course, getting on a day boat at the last minute is a difficult thing to figure out. No matter how late you embark, there is always a wait of twenty minutes before the thing starts, a wait with no breeze in the broiling sun to the accompanying rumble of outbound freight. I have not the statistics at hand, but I venture to say that no boat of less than 4,000 tons ever sailed on time. The captain always has to have an extra cup of coffee up at the Greek's, or a piece of freight gets caught against a stanchion or the engineer can't get the fire to catch. The initial rush to get on board and the scuffle to get seats is followed by a great deal of tooting and ringing of bells—and then a long wait. People who have called out frantic good-bys find themselves involved in what seems to be an endless and footless conversation over the rail which drags on through remarks such as "Don't get seasick" and "Tell mother not to worry" into a forced interchange of flat comments which would hardly have served for the basis of any conversation on shore. It finally ends by the relatives and friends on the pier being the first to leave. The *voyageurs* then return dispiritedly to their seats and bake until the thing sails. Thus, before the trip has even begun, the let-down has set in.

It has always been my theory that the collapsible chairs on a day boat are put out by one firm, the founders of which were the Borgias of medieval Italy. In the old sadistic days, the victim was probably put into one of these and tied so that he could not get out. Within two hours' time the wooden crosspiece on the back would have forced its way into his body just below the shoulder blades, while the two upright knobs at the corners of the seat would have destroyed his thigh bones, thereby making any further torture, such as the Iron Maiden or the thumbscrews, unnecessary. Today, the steamboat company does not go so far as to tie its victims in, but it gives them no other place to sit on deck, and the only way in which a comfortable reading posture can be struck is for the passenger to lie sideways across the seat with his left arm abaft the crossbar and his left hip resting on the cloth. The legs are then either stretched out straight or entwined around another chair. Sometimes one can be comfortable for as long as four minutes in this position. The best way is to lie down flat on the deck and let people walk over you.

This deliberate construction of chairs to make sitting impossible would be understandable if there were any particular portion of the boat, such as a good lunch counter, to which the company wanted to drive its patrons. But the lunch counters on day boats seem to be run on the theory that Americans, as a nation, eat too much. Ham, Swiss cheese, and, on the dressier boats, tongue sandwiches constitute the *carte du jour* for those who, driven from their seats by impending curvature of the spine, rush to the lunch counter. If the boat happens to be plying between points in New England, that "vacation-land of America," where the business slogan is "The customer is always in the way," the customer is lucky if the chef in attendance furnishes grudgingly a loaf of bread and a piece of ham for him to make his own sandwiches. And a warm bottle of "tonic" is considered all that any epicure could demand as liquid refreshment.

All this would not be so bad if, shortly after the boat starts, a delicious aroma of cooking onions and bacon were not wafted up through the ventilators, which turns out to be coming from the galley where the crew's mid-day meal is being prepared.

If the boat happens to be a "night boat" there is a whole new set of experiences in store for the traveler.

"Don't run so hard, Ethel; you'll tire yourself all out!"

Boarding at about five or six in the afternoon, he discovers that, owing to the Eastern Star or the Wagumsett having been lying alongside the dock all day in the broiling sun, the staterooms are uninhabitable until the boat has been out a good two hours. Even then he has a choice of putting his bags in or getting in himself. A good way to solve this problem is to take the bags with him into one of the lifeboats and spend the night there. Of course, if there are small children in the party (and there always are) two lifeboats will be needed.

Children on a night boat seem to be built of hardier stock than children on any other mode of conveyance. They stay awake later, get up earlier, and are heavier on their feet. If, by the use of sedatives, the traveler finally succeeds in getting to sleep himself along about 3 A.M., he is awakened sharp at four by foot races along the deck outside which seem to be participated in by the combined backfields of Notre Dame and the University of Southern California. Two children can give this effect. Two children and one admonitory parent calling out, "Don't run so hard, Ethel; you'll tire yourself all out!" can successfully bring the half-slumbering traveler to an upright position, crashing his head against the upper bunk with sufficient force to make at least one more hour's unconsciousness possible.

It is not only the children who get up early on these night boats. There is a certain type of citizen who, when he goes on a trip, "doesn't want to miss anything." And so he puts on his clothes at 4:30 A.M. and goes out on deck in the fog. If he would be careful only not to miss anything on the coast line it might not be so bad, but he is also determined not to miss anything in the state-rooms, with the result that sleepers who get through the early-morning childish prattle are bound to be awakened by the uncomfortable feeling that they are being watched. Sometimes, if the sleeper is picturesque enough, there will be a whole family looking in at him, with the youngest child asking, "Is that daddy?" There is nothing left to do but get up and shut the window. And, with the window shut, there is nothing left to do but get out into the air. Thus begins a new day.

Sometime a writer of sea stories will arise who will immortalize this type of travel by water. For it has its heroes and its hardships, to say nothing of its mysteries, and many a good ringing tale could be built around the seamen's yarns now current among the crews of our day and night excursion boats. I would do it myself, but it would necessitate at least a year's apprenticeship and right now I do not feel up to that.

The Tourist Rush

to America

ACCORDING to statistics or whatever you call those long tables of figures with "1929" and "1930" at the tops of the columns, there weren't so many Americans vacationing in Europe last summer as there were the summer before. Of course, it was impossible to get accommodations back to New York on any boat leaving after the middle of August, but that may have been because a lot of Americans adopted Frenchmen and Germans and brought them home. The boats were filled up *some*how. But figures will show that, full boats or not, Americans stayed away from Europe this year in great droves. (I know why, but I am not going to tell. You must guess. It begins with a W and is the name of a street in New York.)

Now, if it is true that American tourist trade to Europe is falling off, then European tourist trade to America will have to begin. There has simply got to be a tourist trade somewhere, otherwise the world will be flooded with picture post cards which nobody will buy and there will be a plague of them.

So far, the only Europeans who have come over here have come to sell something or to lecture. They land in New York, rush right to an import house or lecture platform, do their stuff, and take the next boat back. They very seldom stop to look around, probably because there isn't much to stop to look around at. We have never gone in much for the tourist trade, but, if the future is going to bring great hordes of Europeans to this country to behave as we have been behaving in Europe all these years, we had better begin to look picturesque. We can also begin to jack up prices a bit, having one set of prices for us natives and one for the foreign visitors. Maybe it won't be a pleasure to get one of those French hotel-keepers with a long black mustache into a corner of a real old New England inn with spinning wheels in the lobby and just nick him good and plenty for a sheaf of those little lavender francs he has in his sock!

The boys who hang around the corner drug store are having their pictures taken.

But we shall have to give them something for their money. Not much, perhaps, but a little more than we have to offer now in the way of local color. They will want to see the quaint old streets of Lawrence, Massachusetts, or Portage, Wisconsin. We shall have to make them quaint. They will want to see the natives in native costume. We shall have to rig up something for the residents of Massillon, Ohio, and Denver, Colorado, to wear which will bring forth gasps of delight from our foreign friends—at twenty dollars a gasp.

Of course, some of our citizenry may object to being stared at while they are at their supper, but Americans have been staring at French and German natives for years and it is only fair that they have their chance now. There may be a little trouble if, some warm summer evening, when the Perkinses are sitting out on their front porch getting what breeze there is, a group of French tourists from the local hotel stop and make remarks about Mr. Perkins' suspenders and offer to buy the straw mat out from under Mrs. Perkins as she sits on the steps.

The boys who hang around the corner drug store and make wise cracks at passers-by are going to resent just a bit being pointed out from an automobile-full of Italian visitors as "the lower element of the village, wearing the native headgear," and having their pictures taken by elderly Tyrolese couples who happen to be spending the night in town on their way to Chicago. Mrs. Durkins, on Sycamore Street, isn't going to fancy being interrupted in her housework by having a German artist poke his head in her kitchen window and ask if she will pose for a sketch.

But these things will have to be done if we are going in for getting foreign business. We have made no bones about peering into Dutch windows. We can't object to the Dutch peering into ours. Of course, we *shall* object, but we shouldn't.

In fact, sooner or later we shall probably get used to it and make a little effort to be picturesque. You will find different sections of the country brushing up on the distinctive local dishes and serving them in costume. Our own tea rooms have given us a start on the thing, and in many places the serving of a simple lettuce-and-tomato sandwich involves the dressing up of the waitress like Betsy Ross and the execution of a short minuet by the customer and the cashier.

The step from this sort of thing to catering to foreign visitors is not so drastic. Up around Boston they can put the regular Sunday morning baked beans and fish balls up in little earthenware pots and serve them at a dollar and a half a throw. Everybody in Boston will, I am afraid, have to dress up like Puritans during the summer months, because that is the way that the Europeans will have read about them in their guidebooks. In Philadelphia, scrapple can be elevated to the status of a rare old *vin du pays* and served by Quakeresses or little Ben Franklins. Of course, the South will just drive the foreigners crazy with its famous dishes and local color. It would not be surprising to see corn pone, if dished out by a dear old mammy with a bandanna on, reach an importance where it could draw down three dollars a portion in the open market.

The present batch of guidebooks to points of interest in the United States will have to be revised to make them more like books we get abroad explaining the intricacies of France and Germany, with phrases for use by the foreign traveler. They can be divided up into sections like this:

PHRASES FOR THE STEAMSHIP PIER

What country is this?... That is too bad, I wanted Brazil.... In which direction is the night-club life?... Get the hell out of that trunk!... No, that bottle of cognac is not mine.... I do not know how it got in there.... I am surprised to see that you have discovered yet another bottle of cognac.... They must have been in the trunk when I bought it.... Here, porter, take these bags and my arm.... I want to go first to the corner of Michigan Avenue and Goethe Street, Chicago.

AT THE HOTEL

Please assign me to a room overlooking the Mayor and the City Council. . . . It need not have a bath so long as the bureau drawers are wide enough to accommodate my dress shirts. . . . What shall I write here? . . . How do I know that you will not use my signature to further some nefarious financial coup of your own? Boy, take those three bags of mine and the nice-looking one next to them to Room 1473.

IN THE RESTAURANT

What are your most typical native dishes? . . . Then give me a couple of eggs. . . . I do not care how they are cooked so long as they do not contain sentimental mottoes or confetti. . . . Won't you sit down yourself and have a bite to eat? You seem tired. . . . Perhaps you would like to have *me* serve *you*? . . . What would you like? The chicken pie is very nice today. . . . No, I am *not* nice. I am simply being polite. . . . I would much rather not dance, if you don't mind.

IN THE AVIARY

What type of bird is that? . . . Ugh! . . . Are all three of those one bird, or do they come separately? . . . I am not very crazy about birds. . . . Let us go.

IN THE REPAIR SHOP FOR CIGARETTE LIGHTERS

I would like a new flint for my briquet. . . . I'm sorry, I thought that this was a repair shop for cigarette lighters. . . . Good day.

ON THE WAY BACK TO EUROPE

That is the last time I shall make a voyage to America. . . . Such robbers! . . . I did not see a pretty woman all the time I was there. . . . It will certainly seem good to get back home and have some bad coffee. . . . Well, I suppose everyone ought to see America once, but, for me, give me little old Bucharest every time!

*O*ur
*N*ews-*R*eel *L*ife

WHENEVER we want to find out what life was like in the days of the Pharaohs (when I say "we," I mean people who go in for that sort of thing. Me, I can take it or leave it alone), we have to go all the way to Egypt and dig and dig and dig. And even then, what do we get? A truckload of old signet rings and scarabs, some shawls, and maybe three very unhealthy-looking mummies.

We of the twentieth century are making it lots easier for archæologists of the future to find out what we were like. Whenever they want to rummage around in the past, all they will have to do will be to go to the vault, pull out a dozen tins of news-reels for 1930, and run them off in a cozy projection room. Then they will know all about what we were doing in the days of the Hoover dynasty, what we wore, and how we talked. The only trouble will be that, if they go entirely by the movie news-reels, they may get an impression like the following:

Report on the Manners and Customs of the Inhabitants of America previous to the Great Glacier of 1942-8. Read at a Meeting of the Royal Society of Ultra-Violet Engineers by Prof. Henry Six-Hundred-and-Twelve, custodian of the Motion Picture News-Reels of the British Museum, what there is left of it. Double-April 114th 3738 A.D.

"From the motion-picture news-reels on file in the Museum, it is plain that inhabitants of America in the early decades of the twentieth century were most peculiarly constructed as far as their organs of speech went. Although they moved their lips in talking, as we of today do, the sound cavity or apparatus of articulation seemed to be located somewhere in the region of the collar bone or even as low as the hip. There was a variation of between two and five seconds from the time the words were formed by the lips until the sound issued from the torso, and then it came with great resonance, as if the megaphone were being used.

"This is all very puzzling, for, in the mummies of that period, we are unable to locate any such misplaced speaking apparatus. We have looked everywhere, under the arms, between the ribs, and even in the joints of the elbow, but so far have been able to discover traces of nothing but arms, ribs, and elbows.

"From the news-reels (and other sound pictures) we are able to gather that inanimate objects of that period had distinctive sounds of their own, now happily toned down through ages of refinement. For example, a small piece of paper, on being folded, gave off a sound comparable to the crashing of one of our giant redwoods. A door, no matter how easily closed, banged like a trench mortar. A button dropping on the floor sounded as if a large, wet seal had flopped in its tracks. Nothing was too small to make a loud noise.

"The people who inhabited North America at the time we are studying seemed always to be diving from spring-boards, doubtless because of the intense heat of the world at that particular period of its incubation. Practically every news-reel shows us one or more unclad citizens leaping from a board into the water, a maneuver which also gave off a horrendous sound much louder than our modern water. A feature of this diving was the stationing of off-stage characters to shout what must have then been considered witty remarks at the divers, such as, 'How's the water, Bill?' One hears the voices but seldom sees the speakers —which is probably just as well.

"Public speakers of that time were not particularly proficient in the art of oratory, or, at any rate, not before the microphone, for they always seemed to be confined to notes which were held just out of view of the camera, somewhere in the vicinity of the speaker's instep. Reading under these difficulties made it necessary for the orator to keep his head down and his eyes lowered, with the result that usually the bald spot on the top of his head was all that was visible. And even then he quite often forgot what he was about to say, or lost his place, making a highly unsatisfactory event of the thing. We would deplore this inaccuracy more if it were not for the fact that the speakers, when they *could* be understood, rarely seemed to be saying anything worth hearing. As historical evidence they are practically worthless.

"While we are on the subject of public speakers of that era, it might be well to point out that, almost without exception, they wore a type of linen collar which, even in 1930, was old-fashioned. The curator of our Collar Department has identified it as a turnover collar of the 1908–10 age, which comes together in a straight up-and-down line in front and gives every indication of choking the wearer. Nobody as late as 1930, except politicians, ever wore them, but, as President Weaver (or Hoever), the Chief Executive at that time, had a penchant for these affairs, it is possible that the rest wore them as a mark of allegiance to the Republican (or Democratic, as it was sometimes called) party.

"For a country as provincial as the United States was at this time, the news-reel displayed a remarkable interest in Japanese and Korean school children. Almost every film that we have in our possession shows Japanese and Korean school children in some form of intellectual activity, such as reciting in unison, 'Out of the window you must go!' or grouping themselves to form the letters of the word, 'WALCOME.'

"We are also at a loss to understand just how the world's supply of petroleum was ever garnered, for every oil tank

Usually the bald spot on the top of his head was all that was visible.

The turnover collar, which gives every indication of choking the wearer.

This sort of thing may very well have been a form of folk dancing.

or oil well in America was always on fire. There must have been *some* which did not send out great volumes of black smoke at all times, but we have no record of them in the movies. It is barely possible that the quality of oil drawn from the ground in that era was of such a specific gravity that a certain boiling or toasting was necessary before it could be used, but it would seem that this great period of oil conflagration was the prelude to the final exhaustion of the oil supply in the southern part of the country and its discovery under the surface of what was then the island of Manhattan, now happily given over to oil wells.

"The 1930 news-reels are a splendid source of information for the present-day tacticians in their supply of pictures showing the 'floating fort' or 'battleship' of the day. There seems to have been little use for these cumbersome engines of warfare except to shoot off guns in front of movie cameras. There would be a puff of smoke, followed some seconds later by a vague booming sound, with a concurrent blare of band music playing a tune which research leads us to believe was known as Sail, Navy, Down the Field. The crews of these ships trained for warfare by sitting astride the large guns and swaying back and forth in time to the music.

"The games of that age were evidently concerned more with running in all directions than our present-day games of intensive manual skill. Almost every shred of evidence which we have shows more or less shadowy men dashing back and forth in front of the camera, either after striking in the air with a stick or catching an object about the size of a man's head. At times, two men would get together under brilliant lights and hold each other's shoulders, rocking back and forth until one or the other had smothered his opponent, but this sort of thing may very well have been a form of folk dancing and not a sport. The pictures are very hazy at best, and we are unable to form any accurate judgment of just what the technique of all these games was.

"It was at this time that flying was in its initial stages and we have ample sources from which to draw our conclusions about the manner in which it was done. Hundreds of moving pictures are at our disposal showing a terrifically noisy preliminary agitation in what must have been the motor compartment (motors were used almost exclusively at that time, although there were some motorless planes called gliders which received an abnormal amount of publicity), followed by a flash of more or less formless shadow and something disappearing into the air. It is hard to imagine such public interest in an activity as natural as flying, but great crowds would sometimes assemble at the take-off or landing, and the one who was making the flight would at times deliver a short speech saying that he had every intention of reaching his destination.

"All of these films are readily accessible to those students of archæology who are interested in the period under discussion and, on application at the registrar's office, will be shown gladly. Except to postgraduate students, however, they are not very interesting."

*L*ittle

*N*oise *A*batement

So now we are to have no more noise. Scientific research has disclosed the fact that the effect of harsh noises on the brain is more deleterious than that of drugs, and nowhere near so pleasant while it is happening. The bursting of a paper bag, according to the Noise Abatement Commission, increases the brain pressure more than does morphine, but you don't read of anyone smuggling paper bags into the country just to bang them in some addict's ear at so much per bang. Noise is bad for you and isn't even any fun. It's a wonder that they care about prohibiting it.

Doing away with banging paper bags is a good beginning, along with sidewalk loud-speakers and other public disturbers, but why not first do away with the people who think it is funny to bang paper bags? You would find that you were killing about 500 birds with one stone, for they are the ones who make almost all other kinds of obnoxious noises. Anyone who thinks it is funny to sneak up behind you and whack an inflated paper bag (and is there anything more satisfactory than to see the chagrin on his face when the bag turns out to be a dud and refuses to bang?) will also sneak up behind you and push you off rafts into the water, will dive down and grab your legs while you are swimming, will snap rubber bands at you, and will cover his lower teeth with his lip and emit piercing whistles. Get rid of one and you will have got rid of them all.

This shrill whistling through the teeth is a sure indication in a boy that he will grow up to be an obnoxious citizen. They usually practice it in public gatherings where it will attract attention to themselves. It is offered in place of any mental attainment or physical prowess and is almost always the mark of retarded development along lines other than whistling through the teeth. In a crowd, if you will watch carefully, you will see the boy who has just whistled himself into prominence sooner or later will begin to push. This is also considered funny, especially if a good flying wedge can be started which will knock over a couple of old ladies. It is all a part of the banging-paper-bags and whistling-through-the-teeth psychology and is, mental experts will tell you, the sign of an inferiority complex. Inferiority is a mild word for it.

What the scientists do not seem to have taken into consideration in their researches is that it is not so much the noise itself that irritates as the knowledge that someone is making the noise deliberately.

That it is entirely a question of whether the noise is necessary or not is shown by the fact that I am not upset by the sound of celery or nuts being eaten. There is no way that I know of, unless they are ground up into a paste and dissolved in the mouth, by which celery and nuts can be eaten noiselessly. So my nerves get a rest during this course, and I have nothing but the kindliest feelings toward the eater. In fact, I don't hear it at all. But ice-crunching and loud gum-chewing, together with drumming on tables and whistling the same tune seventy times in succession, because they indicate an indifference on the part of the perpetrator to the rest of the world in general, are not only registered on the delicate surface of the brain but eat little holes in it until it finally collapses or blows up. I didn't see this mentioned anywhere in the Commission's report.

The Commission, in fact, just concentrates on the big noises, like those which go to make up what poets call "the symphony of a big city." Some of these are also the

My nerves get a rest during this course.

result of the activities of grownups who used to whistle through their teeth when they were boys and who now don't care how much they disturb other people so long as they call attention to themselves. In this class are those owners of radio supply shops who stick big horns out over their doors to give the Maine Stein Song an airing from nine to six every day; chauffeurs who sound their horns in a traffic jam when they know that it will do no good; and, I am sorry to say, mendicants who walk up and down the street playing shrill little instruments featuring The Blue Danube Waltz and Happy Days in rotation.

I hate to be nasty about blind men (if they really are blind) but there is one who takes up a stand right under my window on Tuesdays, Thursdays, and Saturdays and plays a clarinet most of the afternoon. He is accompanied by a helper with a banjo.

Now, a clarinet is an instrument with considerable volume and powerful reach. It sounds out above the noise of the elevator (which I don't mind) and the riveting (which I can make allowances for) and the worst of it is he plays it pretty well. When it first begins I rather enjoy it.

I stop my lathe and hum softly to myself. I sometimes even get up and execute a short *pas seul* if nobody is looking. But his repertory is limited, and, after a while, I'm Dancing with Tears in My Eyes Because the Girl in My Arms Isn't You loses its sentimental value and begins its work on my nerve fibers. I try to say to myself: "Come, come, the man is blind and very poor," but then I remember reading about street beggars who not only are really not blind but who make more in a day than I do in some weeks (this week, for instance) and I become convinced that this man is one of those. And why can't he move on? Doesn't he ever stop to think that there are probably 5,000 people who are being driven mad by his music within a radius of one block? Aren't there *any* instruments that he can play which aren't so loud? By this time I am in a rage which is cumulative every time he stops and I hear him begin again. (The stopping and beginning again is really the peak of the irritation.) The whole thing ends in my shutting all the windows and getting under the bed to sulk.

I hope that the Noise Abatement Commission will take cognizance of these things. If they don't, I have my own resources. I have a small rifle with which I am practicing every day at a shooting gallery, and I am going to try it out on that newsboy (aged thirty-five, with a voice to match) who picks out the noon hour about once a week to walk through my street announcing that "Nya-a-ya-nyaded! Onoy-naded!" in tones which would indicate that he has three other men inside him. I may not wait for the Noise Abatement Commission to get him.

As a matter of fact, I have every confidence that some of the louder and more general noises will be abated. It is the little noises that I am after, or rather the people who make the little noises. My brain cells are pretty far gone as it is, but it may not be too late. Of course, the question might arise as to what I shall use my brain for, once I have saved it. There will be time enough to figure that out when the noises have stopped.

"Accustomed

as I Am—"

It can't really be that there are fewer banquets being held than in the old days. It is probably that I myself am attending fewer. I know that was my intention several years ago, and I must be living up to it. It makes me very proud to think that at least one thing that I set out to do in my life I have done. I have attended fewer banquets.

But, just as when your own headache stops you think that there are no such things as headaches in the world, so now that I have stopped going to banquets it seems to me that the practice is dying out. I see notices in the newspapers that a testimonial dinner has been given to Lucius J. Geeney, or that the convening salesmen of the A.A.O.U.A.A.A. have got together for one final address by the "Big Boss" over the coffee cups filled with cigarette ends, but I don't read them. Oh, *how* I don't read them! I should say that there was no reading matter in the world, including the Koran in the original, which is so unread by me as the newspaper accounts of banquet speeches. But they tell me that, even under this handicap, they are still going on.

The bitterness on my part arises from two rather dark splotches in my past. I used to be a newspaper reporter, and, not being a particularly valuable one, I was sent every night to cover whatever banquet there might be at the old Waldorf or at the Astor. My records show that I attended ninety-two banquets in one winter, which meant that I listened to about three hundred and sixty-eight after-dinner speeches during that time, all of them beginning "I shall not take much of your time tonight," and ending, forty-five minutes later, with "but I have already taken too much of your time."

Finally, unable to control myself any longer, I began mocking after-dinner speakers. I worked up some after-dinner speeches of my own, built along the conventional lines, and wormed my way into banquet programs, where I would deliver them in hopes of offending some of the old boys who had tortured me for so long. But, instead of flying into a rage, they drafted me into their ranks, and the first thing I knew, instead of waging war on after-dinner speakers I found that I was one myself! Tie that for irony!

It took me quite a long time to realize that I was actually a professional banqueteer and not an amateur crusader against banquets. I began to suspect the truth when I started getting letters from chairmen of banquet committees in Pennsylvania or Missouri suggesting that I come and make a speech before the Men's Club of the Rumbold Association or at the annual dinner of the Assistant Bankers' Club, adding: "We haven't very much money in our treasury, but you would be our guest for the duration of your stay in town and we can assure you of a royal good time." Then I knew that I was really a member of the Journeymen Talkers, and a great flush of shame swept my brow. I was hoist by my own, or, at any rate, a borrowed petard.

Imagine my predicament. (All right, *don't* then! I'll tell it to you.) Having stood all the after-dinner speeches that I could as a reporter, I now had to listen to a lot more, including my own. I tried to make mine so insulting that I would be thrown out of the union. I tried to impress it on my brothers in the bond of boredom that I was *against* them and not with them. But they were so busy running over their own speeches in their minds, or so firmly convinced that what they had just said was beyond being kidded, that water on a duck's back was a permanent institution compared with my weak lampoons. It was then that I admitted myself licked, and withdrew from the field.

But, during my brief membership in the ranks of the Coldstream Guards, I learned to have a little pity for them in their chosen calling. Not much, but a little. They have a pretty tough fight at times. Of course, they wouldn't be making speeches if they didn't want to (the exceptions being those poor wretches who get roped into the thing against their wills and bend four coffee spoons and crumble up eight bits of bread in terror before they are called upon), but also entertainment committees wouldn't have asked them if they weren't wanted. So the entertainment committees are equally to blame and probably more so. Now that we have got rid of the open saloon, I recommend that we get rid of all entertainment committees. They are a menace to the nation.

Granted that the speaker has been asked, even urged, to make a speech. Granted that he really loves doing it. What does he do for his money besides bore the living life out of his audience? He has to eat broiled jumbo squab *bonne femme*, combination salad *Henri*, and raspberry *baiser* in a paper cuff, talking with a strange master of ceremonies at his left who is so nervous about his part of the program that he eats his notes instead of his celery and gives the impression of being very cross with the guest. He (the speaker) is asked, at the last minute, by someone who comes up behind his chair enveloped in an aroma of rye, to insert in his speech some funny crack at Harry Pastwick, P-a-s-t-w-i-c-k, who has just been appointed Sales Manager. He is introduced by the nervous master of ceremonies as somebody else or in terms which indicate that the master of ceremonies is only vaguely familiar with his name and record and cares less. And then he begins his speech.

That is, he begins as soon as thirty or thirty-five guests have scraped their way out of the banquet hall to the gentlemen's room, and thirty or thirty-five more have scraped their way back to their seats. He begins as soon as the boys at Table 48 in the back of the room have stopped singing Kentucky Moon, and as soon as the representative from the Third Sales District has been convinced that if he stays under the table he will catch cold. And he begins without waiting for the waiters to get fifteen hundred coffee cups quiet.

"Mr. Chairman, fellow guests, members of the American Association of Aromatics: When your chairman asked me to speak to you tonight, I felt somewhat in the position of the Scotchman who, when asked—"

At this point one of the members, probably technically in the right, but distinctly out of order, yells, "Louder and funnier!" There is probably no more devastating or

"Louder and funnier!"

bloodcurdling cry in the world to a man who is on his feet trying to make a speech. There can be no answer, only a sickly smile. A sensitive man will sit down then and there, but sensitive men aren't usually up making speeches. As for the man who yells "Louder and funnier!" he ought to be made to get up himself and be funny. The only trouble is that he probably would love it.

I realize that this isn't much punishment to subject a man to for talking forty minutes overtime, but, as I figure it out, both sides get only what is coming to them. The speaker knows what he is in for when he agrees to make a speech. And if the banqueteers, after all the experience they have had, don't know what they are in for when they attend a banquet, then they deserve what they are getting. This thing has been going on for years. It has always been the same, and it probably always will be. Very young boys may be excused and pitied for attending their first banquet, but after that, they have nobody but themselves to blame.

Look at me. I stopped going, and see how happy I am!

Back in Line

FOR a nation which has an almost evil reputation for bustle, bustle, bustle, and rush, rush, rush, we spend an enormous amount of time standing around in line in front of windows, just waiting. It would be all right if we were Spanish peasants and could strum guitars and hum, or even stab each other, while we were standing in line, or East Indians who could just sit cross-legged and simply stare into space for hours. Nobody expects anything more of Spanish peasants or East Indians, because they have been smart enough to build themselves a reputation for picturesque lethargy.

But we in America have built ourselves reputations for speed and dash, and are known far and wide as the rushingest nation in the world. So when fifty of us get in a line and stand for an hour shifting from one foot to the other, rereading the shipping news and cooking recipes in an old newspaper until our turn comes, we just make ourselves look silly.

Most of this line-standing is the fault of the Government, just as everything else which is bad in our national life is the fault of the Government, including stone bruises and tight shoes. We would have plenty of time to rush around as we are supposed to do, if the Government did not require 500 of us to stand in one line at once waiting for two civil service employees to weigh our letters, thumb out income-tax blanks, tear off our customs slips or roll back our eyelids. Of course, there are times when we stand in line to see a ball game or buy a railroad ticket, but that is *our* affair, and in time we get enough sense to stop going to ball games or traveling on railroads.

The U.S. Post Office is one of the most popular line-standing fields in the country. It has been estimated that six-tenths of the population of the United States spend their entire lives standing in line in a post office. When you realize that no provision is made for their eating or sleeping or intellectual advancement while they are thus standing in line, you will understand why six-tenths of the population look so cross and peaked. The wonder is that they have the courage to go on living at all.

This congestion in the post offices is due to what are technically known as "regulations" but what are really a series of acrostics and anagrams devised by some officials who got around a table one night and tried to be funny. "Here's a good gag!" one of them probably cried. "Let's make it so that as soon as a customer reaches the window with his package after his forty-five minutes in line, he has to go home again, touch some object made of wood, turn around three times, and then come back and stand in line again!" "No, no, that's too easy!" another objected. "Let's make it compulsory for the package to be wrapped in paper which is watermarked with Napoleon's coat of arms. We won't say anything about it until they get right up to the window, so there will be no danger of their bringing that kind of paper with them. Then they will have to go away again with their bundles, find some paper watermarked with Napoleon's coat of arms (of which there is none that I ever heard of), rewrap their bundles, and come back and stand in line again. What do you say to that!" This scheme probably threw the little group of officials into such a gale of merriment that they had to call the meeting off and send down for some more White Rock.

You can't tell me that the post-office regulations (to say nothing of those of the Custom House and Income Tax Bureau) were made with anything else in mind except general confusion. It must be a source of great chagrin to those in charge to think of so many people being able to stick a stamp on a letter and drop it into a mail box without any trouble or suffering at all. They are probably working on that problem at this very minute, trying to devise some way in which the public can be made to fill out a blank, stand in line, consult some underling who will refer them to a superior, and then be made to black up with burned cork before they can mail a letter. And they'll figure it out, too. They always have.

But at present their chief source of amusement is in torturing those unfortunates who find themselves with a package to send by mail. And with Christmas in the offing, they must be licking their chops with glee in very anticipation. Although bundles of old unpaid bills is about all anyone will be sending this Christmas, it doesn't make any difference to the P.O. Department. A package is a package, and you must suffer for it.

The wonder is that they have the courage to go on living at all.

It wouldn't be a bad idea for those of us who have been through the fire to get together and cheat the officials out of their fun this year by sending out lists of instructions (based on our own experience) to all our friends, telling them just what they have got to look out for before they start to stand in line. Can you imagine the expression on the face of a post-office clerk if a whole line of people came up to his window, one by one, each with his package so correctly done up that there was no fault to find with it? He would probably shoot himself in the end, rather than face his superiors with the confession that he had sent no one home to do the whole thing over. And if his superiors shot themselves too it would not detract one whit from the joyousness of the Christmas tide.

So here are the things I have learned in my various visits to the Post Office. If you will send me yours and get ten friends to make a round robin of their experiences, we may thwart the old Government yet.

Packages to be mailed abroad must be:

1. Wrapped in small separate packages, each weighing no more than one pound and seven-eighths (Eastern Standard Time), and each package to be tied with blue ribbon in a sheepshank knot. (Any sailor of fifteen years' experience will teach you to tie a sheepshank.)

2. The address must be picked out in blue, and re-enforced with an insertion of blue ribbon, no narrower than three-eighths of an inch and no wider than five-eighths of an inch, (and certainly not exactly four-eighths or one-half), or else you may have to stay and write it out a hundred times after the post office has closed.

3. The package, no matter what size, will have to be made smaller.

4. The package, no matter what size, will have to be made larger.

(In order to thwart the clerk on these last two points, it will be necessary to have packages of *all* sizes concealed in a bag slung over your back.)

5. The person who is mailing the package must approach

the window with the package held in his right hand extended toward the clerk one foot from the body, while with the left hand he must carry a small bunch of lilies of the valley, with a tag on them reading: "Love from—[name of sender]—to the U.S. Post Office."

6. The following ritual will then be adhered to, a deviation by a single word subjecting the sender to a year in Leavenworth or both:

Clerk's Question: Do you want to mail a package?
Sender's Answer: No, sir.
Q. What *do* you want to do?
A. I don't much care, so long as I can be with you.
Q. Do you like tick-tack-toe?
A. I'm crazy mad for it.
Q. Very well. We won't play that.
A. Aren't you being just a little bit petty?
Q. Are you criticizing *me*?
A. Sorry.
Q. And high time. Now what do you want?
A. *You,* dear.
Q. You get along with yourself. What's in your hand?
A. Flowers for you—*dear.*
Q. I know that. What's in the other hand?
A. I won't tell.
Q. Give it here this minute.
A. You won't like it.
Q. Give-it-here-this-minute, I say.
The sender reluctantly gives over the parcel.
Q. What do you want to do with this?
A. I want to take it home with me and wrap it up again.
Q. You leave it here, and *like it.*
A. Please give it back. Please, pretty please?
Q. I will do no such thing. You leave it here and I will mail it for you. And shut up!

The sender leaves the window, sobbing. The clerk, just to be mean, mails the package.

A *B*rief *C*ourse in
*W*orld *P*olitics

THERE used to be a time when anyone could keep in touch with the world's history (if anyone was fool enough to want to) by consulting Rand, McNally's map or by remembering that, no matter what country it was, there were only two things that could happen: either the king could have some people beheaded, or some people could have the king beheaded. It was all very simple and cozy.

But the Great War, in addition to making the old Rand, McNally's map look like an early American sampler with "God Bless Our Home" sewn on it, and in addition to making the average man's income look like what you find in the pocket of last winter's suit, also made it a great deal more difficult to follow subsequent changes in political parties throughout the world. It has become so complicated that it is hardly worth the trouble. Beyond a certain point the thing loses interest.

For example, we read one day in the newspapers that Germany has gone over from the control of the Workers National Peoples Socialist Centrist Party (with 256 seats) to the Bavarian Nationalist Optimist Fascist Unreinigung Party (with 396 seats), which means that trouble is brewing all over the map of Europe. Now, try as you will, it is difficult to understand this. Especially as the next day you read that the election which hurled the Workers Nationalist Optimist Centrist, etc., people into office, was a preliminary election or *Wahl*, and that the finals have shown that the balance of power resides in the hands of the Christian Hanoverian Revalorization Gesellschaft Party (with fifteen seats and a bicycle), which means that Europe is on the verge of a conflagration, beginning with a definite rupture with the Slovenes (the Extreme Left Slovenes, that is, not to be confused with the Conservative Radical Slovenes).

Republicans and Democrats I can understand, but I don't care. Liberals and Conservatives are an open book to me; one is liberal, the other conservative, or vice versa. But when you get twenty-four parties, all beginning with "W," on each one of which the future peace of Europe depends, then I am sorry but I shall have to let Europe figure it out for itself and let me know when it is going to have another war. That is, if it can find me. I still can run pretty fast.

I try to keep up with the political parties of Germany because I am very partial to German food and whatever that stuff is they serve with it. But keeping track of China is something that I can't, and won't, do. Anyone who tries to keep track of what is happening in China is going to end up by wearing all the skin off his left ear from twirling around on it. The only way to follow the various revolutions and army maneuvers in China is to throw yourself on your face on the floor and kick and scream until some Chinese expert comes and explains them to you. Not a *Chinese* expert really, but an American expert on China. A Chinese expert would only serve to confuse you the more.

You simply can't get anything out of China by reading the newspapers or the weeklies. I doubt very much if the newspapers and weeklies can get anything out of China themselves. For, in China, not only do they change parties every twelve minutes, but the parties themselves keep changing. The Northern Army, under Wu Wing Chang, will suddenly, without warning, became the Southern Army under Li Hung Chu. You may follow the Peiping forces, in their victorious march up the left bank of the Yangtze-Kiang and then, on Tuesday morning, read that somebody has blown a whistle, that the soldiers have pulled little strings in their uniforms, changing them from red to robin's-egg blue, and that Wu Wing Chang has turned into somebody named Arthur McKeever Chamison of Oak Bluffs, Massachusetts. The last man I knew who tried to follow the Chinese armies ended up by picking little spots of light off walls and putting them in a basket.

Then there is South America. Or perhaps we should say, there *was* South America. A lot of jokes have been made about South American revolutions and their frequency, but it isn't the frequency so much that is disturbing as it is their going around all sounding alike. It really makes very little difference to me whether the cabinet of Dr. Huijos or the cabinet of General Yrobarja is in power, but I don't like to pick up my paper and find that Dr. Huijos is General Yrobarja. That, frankly, does confuse me, and I resent being confused, especially after I have been following a thing very carefully from one day to another. There must be a lot of activity going on during the night in those South American revolutions, activity that never gets into the papers. Otherwise it wouldn't be possible for one party to be in power right after the salad course at dinner and another one in power, without so much as a word to the referee, before breakfast the next day. *Some*thing goes on during the night—they change hats, or something—and I personally don't like the looks of the thing at all.

Of course, I did get a little needlessly confused over a revolution they had down there some months ago, and I am perfectly willing to admit that it was my fault. I forgot for the minute and thought that Peru was the capital of the Argentine. You can see how that would tie things up a bit in my mind. One day the revolution in the Argentine was settled and the next day it was at its peak in Peru, with no mention (naturally enough, as I later realized) of what I had read the day before about Argentina. "What is this?" was the way I phrased it to myself. One day President Leguia was thrown out and the next day President Irigoyen (who, up to this time, had taken no part in the conversation) was thrown out. And all through it ran someone named President

Something goes on during the night—they change hats, or something.

Uriburu. "Maybe I missed the papers one day," I thought. "Maybe I slept through Friday." It was in checking up on this end of it that I came across some items which recalled to my mind that Peru is one country and the Argentine is another, and that cleared up the whole ugly mess for me. When I say "cleared up" I mean nothing of the sort.

It is this sort of thing going on all over the world which makes it so difficult for a sincere student of *Weltpolitik*. The country I like best is Sweden. They have a nice king, who shows up every once in a while in the news reels, so you can keep an eye on him. They may have Centrist and Double-Centrist parties, and, in their own quiet way, they may fight out certain issues among themselves, but there is none of this "Overthrow of Cabinet Upsets World's Balance of Power" or "New Alignment in Ingeborg Menaces Europe's Peace." I would like to bet that they have two parties, the Harvards and the Yales, or the Blue and the Gray, and that when one party is in power the other is making snowballs to throw. That is the way the whole world should be, if you will pardon my making a suggestion.

As it stands now, I am likely to throw the whole thing up and go in for contract bridge. There, at least, you know who your partner is. You may not act as if you knew, and your partner may have grave doubts about you ever knowing, but, in your own mind, the issues are very clearly defined. And that is a lot more than you can say of the world today. (A list of what you *can* say for the world today will be found tucked away in a stamp box in the upper left-hand drawer of my desk. It may be stuck to the under side of one of the stamps, but it should be there.)

"$\mathcal{H}$ere You $\mathcal{A}$re—
Taxi!"

It looks now, or rather it did the last time I looked, as if taxicabs in New York were going to be all put under one management and one franchise, like gas mains and trolley cars. Before this plan goes into effect, I have a few words that I would like to say to the Committee in Charge. If the members of the Committee wish, they may leave the room while I am talking.

I want taxicabs to be more standardized. I want to know, when I hail a cab at night, just what sort of conveyance it is that I am going to get into. Many's the time I have stepped out into the street on a dark night all dressed up in my pretty things and raised my gold-headed cane with an imperious gesture signifying that I am ready, nay eager, to be carried somewhere in considerable splendor, only to find, on entering the first cab which stops for me, that I am in the old sleigh which used to stand up in the attic at Grandpa's barn in Millbury. How they ever got it down to New York I don't know.

I know that it is Grandpa's old sleigh by the musty smell inside. If you can tell me why some taxicabs, with motors and exhaust pipes and complete transmissions, should smell of horses and old oats and ancient whip sockets, I will—well, I will be much obliged. (A pretty weak return for all your trouble, I realize.) I have found myself in so-called taxicabs whose heavy plush seats, with nice big holes in the middle

in which to hide from the other boys, have had every acces-
sory of the old-time surrey except the horse. And the horse
had been there only a few hours before, I am sure. Sometimes
there is even a lap robe, one of those old gray lap robes
which, on being unfolded, always were found to contain a
handful of corn kernels and some bits of leghorn fluff. What
I want to know is, are these really old surreys which have
had motors installed, or is it all my imagination and am I
going through a form of second childhood? If it is the latter,
I want to do something about it right away before it goes any
farther. Otherwise I may start clucking at an imaginary
horse before long.

This is the sort of thing that I want to avoid when they
get around to standardizing taxicabs. I want to have it so
that I can hail a cab at night and not be taken for a straw
ride. I want to know what it is that I am getting into.

Of course, you can always count on finding yourself in
one of these musty ghosts of an elder day if you take one of
the cabs forced on you by the doorman at any of our most
exclusive hotels. We call ourselves a free nation, and yet
we let ourselves be told what cabs we can and can't take
by a man at a hotel door, simply because he has a drum
major's uniform on. The ritzier the hotel, the worse, and
the more expensive, are the cabs standing in its own hack
stand, and if you try to hail a passing cab which looks as if
it might have been built after 1900, the doorman will be
very, very cross with you and make you go back into the
hotel and come out again all over. I once got quite indepen-
dent when a doorman told me that I couldn't take the cab
I wanted and I stepped out into the street to take it, his
orders to the contrary notwithstanding. The only trouble
with my revolution was that the cab I wanted hadn't seen
me hail it and drove right by, and I was left standing in two
inches of slush with nothing at all to ride in. So I had to
make believe that I was going across the street anyway, a
process which almost resulted in complete annihilation and
in losing one shoe.

If all the taxis were the same, there would not be this constant struggling back and forth with doormen, for it wouldn't make any difference which cab you took. Or, rather, the only difference would be in the drivers.

Taxi drivers are always going to differ, I suppose, whether the state runs the business or not, but there might be some way of showing a prospective fare just what the personality of his driver is going to be. A red light on the starboard side could mean that the chauffeur is conversationally inclined, a green light that he would rather be left to himself. I, personally, prefer the conversational kind as a general rule, but there might be times when I wanted to do some reading or take a tardy shave, and then a good, quiet, even sullen, companion would be appreciated. On the whole, though, I have found taxi drivers to be much more consistently agreeable and sensitive to your wishes than any other class of the citizenry. If you want to talk, they will talk (and very delightfully, too). If you want to sit quietly and sob or read, they sense it and look straight ahead. Find me any other type of person who will do that.

This matter of reading in cabs could stand a little preliminary planning, too. Reading in a cab at night is bad enough, for, after groping up and down the sides and pushing screws and hinges and ineffectual protuberances in a search for the tiny light switch, it is nine times out of ten discovered that the light doesn't work, or that it goes on only when the door is opened.

And you can't go whizzing through the streets with a door swinging open just to find out who won the football game.

But in the daytime it is much more tantalizing to try and catch a few paragraphs between jounces, for you think that the windows are going to be some help in letting in light—and they are not. You try to hold the paper up to the little back window, with your head twisted off to the right to avoid a shadow, but that doesn't give *quite* enough light to get beyond the headlines. You then try leaning over toward one of the door windows, but that necessitates getting halfway off

. . . only to find it already occupied by people who do not want to see me at that particular time.

the seat and leaves you in no position at all to cope with the next jounce. I have a scar on one of my cheekbones to this day resulting from a nasty reading wound incurred while trying to hold a paper where I could see it just as we went over an uncovered water main.

All of this could be remedied, if the new scheme goes through, by a little care in the construction of cabs and perhaps a poll of patrons giving suggestions.

Aside from the installation of reading lamps and character guides to drivers' personal traits, I would like to offer the following list of possible accessories which would make it easier for us to hail a taxi and ride in it with a certain degree of comfort:

(1) A light on top reading "Taxi," so that I shall not constantly be hailing private cars and incurring the displeasure of their owners.

(2) Another light reading "Taken" or "Not to Be Disturbed until 9 A.M.," so that I shall not snatch open the

door of a stalled cab only to find it already occupied by people who do not want to see me at that particular time.

(3) Some elevation of the door frame which will make it possible to enter a cab wearing a tall hat without having to go back immediately for a new one.

(4) Little hooks on which tall hats or derbies may be hung to avoid having them jammed over the ears by contact with roofs when going over bumps.

(5) Special helicopter attachment on the roof, making it possible for a cab stuck in traffic to rise, fly over the blockade, and land where it will have some chance of reaching its destination.

Or perhaps it would be simpler just not to use taxicabs at all.

*I*nherent *V*ice:
*E*xpress *P*aid

=====

SOME evening, when you haven't anything to read, why not light a cozy fire, draw up your chair, and browse around among your old express receipts and bills of lading? You will learn a lot. Here you have been going on for years, sending parcels and crates like mad, and I'll bet that not one of you really knows the contractual obligations you have been entering into with the companies who serve you. For all you know, you have been agreeing to marry the company manager at the end of sixty days.

As I write this, I am sitting in the gloaming of a late autumn afternoon with an express company's receipt on the table before me. As I read over the fine print on the back of it, my eyes cross gradually with the strain and I put on the light. (What a wonderful invention—electricity! I am sure that we should all be very proud and happy to be living in this age.)

As my eyes adjust themselves, I find that when I sent that old bureau to Ruth's folks, I agreed to let the express company get away with the following exceptions to their liability. (If you are going to read this article, I would advise studying the following. It will probably amuse you more than what I have to say afterward.)

> The company shall in no event be liable for any loss, damage, or delay to said property or to any part thereof occasioned by act of God, by perils or accidents of the sea or other waters, [That

"other waters" makes a pretty broad exemption, when you come to think of it. It means that they can upset tumblers on your stuff, or let roguish employees play squirt guns all over it, and yet not be responsible.] or of navigation or transportation of whatsoever nature or kind; by fire or explosion . . . by theft or pilferage [What about garroting?] by any person whatsoever; by arrest or restraint of governments, princes, rulers, or peoples or those purporting to exercise governmental or other authority; by legal process or stoppage in transit; by fumigation or other acts or requirements of quarantine or sanitary authorities; [Tell me when you are getting tired.] by epidemics, pestilence, riots; or rebellions, by war or any of the dangers incident to a state of war, or by acts of any person or group of persons purporting to wage war or to act as a belligerent; [Come, come, Mr. Express Company—aren't you being just a little bit picayune?] by strikes or stoppage of labor or labor troubles, whether of carrier's employees or others; by unseaworthiness of any vessel, lighter, or other craft whatsoever, [Not even just a teeny-weeny bit of a rowboat?] although existing at the time of shipment on board thereof; . . . by water, [You said that once before.] heating, or the effects of climate, frost, decay, smell, taint, rust, sweat, dampness, mildew, spotting, rain or spray, [Ninety-five-a-hundred-all around my goal are it.] INHERENT VICE, [Remember that one; we're coming back to that later.] drainage, leakage, vermin, improper or insufficient packing, inaccuracies or obliterations, errors, [Why don't they just say "errors" and let it go at that?] nor for the breakage of any fragile articles or damage to any materials consisting of or contained in glass; nor shall this company [Beginning all over again, in case you should have forgotten who it is that isn't responsible.] be held liable or responsible for any damage to or resulting from dangerous corrosives, explosives, or inflammable goods, even if the true nature has been declared to the company; nor for neglect, damage, accident to or escape or mortality of any animals or birds [Ah-ha! They forgot fish!] received by the company hereunder, from any cause whatsoever.

That's all! Aside from that, the express company is responsible for your package.

Aside from that, your little crate or barrel is as safe as it would be in your own home. It would almost be better to get a sled and drag your package yourself to wherever you want it taken.

At least you could personally fight off vermin and princes (or those purporting to be vermin and princes).

But the thing that worries me most about this contract between me and the express company is that clause about "inherent vice."

It would almost be better to get a sled and drag your package to wherever you want it.

The company is not responsible for any damage to that bureau of mine if it is caused by inherent vice. This makes you stop and think.

Wholly aside from the Calvinistic dourness of the phrase "inherent vice" (I thought that the theory of Original Sin and Inherent Vice went out with the hanging of witches), the question now arises—*whose* inherent vice? The company's officials? The bureau's? Aunt Alice's? We are up against quite a nice problem in ethics here.

I can't imagine what you could send by express that would be full enough of inherent vice to damage it en route. Certainly nothing that you could pack in a bureau.

You might send some very naughty rabbits or squirrels by express, but it seems a little narrow-minded to put all the responsibility for their actions on the little creatures themselves. No one has ever told them that they are vicious, or that they were conceived in sin. They don't *know* that they are being bad.

I have known one or two very smart dogs who were pretty self-conscious about being wicked and couldn't look you in the eye afterward, but aside from cases like that it seems a bit arbitrary for a big public-service corporation like an express company to frown on the peccadillos of five or six squirrels.

Would the private lives of the company officials themselves bear looking into so well that they must prate of inherent vice? Live and let live, say I.

Which brings us to the other theory—that inherent vice in the company's officials or employees cannot be held responsible for any damage to my bureau.

Do you mean to tell me that if one of the company's employees is a man who, ever since he was a boy, has been willfully and maliciously destructive, and that if he takes my bureau out of its crate and chops the whole thing up into kindling—do you mean to tell me that I am without recourse to the law?

If the president of the express company or any one of his employees goes monkeying around with my bureau and then pleads "not guilty" because of his inherent vice, I will start a *putsch* that will bring our government crashing down around our cars.

I refuse to discuss the remaining possibility—that the inherent vice referred to means inherent vice in Aunt Alice, or consignee.

This brings us to the conclusion that what is meant is that the package or bale or crate (or articles purporting to be packages, or bales, or crates) might have inherent vice enough to spoil it, and that, in this event, the company washes its hands of the whole affair.

The only alternative to this almost incredibly silly reservation is that there has been a misprint and that what the company is so afraid of is "inherent *mice*." In this case, I have taken up all your time for nothing. But I do think that you ought to know what you are agreeing to when you send an express package. Or perhaps you don't care.

The Helping Hand

I HAVE always tried to be as public-spirited as I could and yet save out a little time to myself for running and jumping. That is, when the Fuel Administration wanted us all to save coal, I saved coal with a will; when it was Anti-Litter Week, I anti-littered; when the nation was supposed to be devoting itself to eating apples, I drank applejack until the cows came home—and very funny-looking cows they were, too.

So when the head of the Unemployment Commission came out over the radio and asked every good citizen to set about "sprucing up" his home and give employment to as many men as possible, I saw my duty and set about doing it.

My house could stand a little "sprucing up," for we have been hoping to sell it for eight or ten years (centrally located in Westchester County, three minutes from the station, colonial type, four master's bedrooms and three masters, servants' quarters at the foot of the plantation, two chimneys, of which one is imitation; just try naming a price and see what happens), and when you expect to sell a house any minute you more or less put off "sprucing up." So I figured that I could help out the situation considerably merely by fixing up the house so that the owls didn't fly in through the roof at night.

Aside from having the roof patted down, I decided that a couple of eaves troughs could stand a little humoring; that one of the master's bathtubs might very well be given a new porcelain filling; that the furnace could easily be looked into by an expert, possibly using a ferret to get out that clinker which got stuck in the grate four years ago; and that we needed a new lock on the front door (or perhaps it was a new key; at any rate, the front door couldn't be locked).

This shaped up like quite a boon to the unemployed of the town. All that remained was for me myself to find enough work to do to pay for it.

We had quite a little trouble in finding a carpenter and a plumber who could promise to come before the following week (no matter how serious the unemployment situation, no individual carpenter or plumber can ever come before the following week, doubtless out of habit), and the lock smith and the furnaceman just didn't seem interested. But we finally got a little group of experts who agreed to drop in the next day and see what could be done.

In the meantime, we had discovered that the electric range needed tampering with and that a fresh coat of paint wouldn't hurt the back porch. So we engaged an electrician and a painter to come in the next day also.

The next day was one of those crisp late fall days when everyone feels so good that he wants to stay right in bed under the blankets all the morning. I was surprised, therefore, in my bathrobe by Mr. Margotson, the carpenter, and Mr. Rallif, the electrician, who arrived together at eight thirty. This started the thing off on an informal basis right at the beginning, and as Mr. Shrank, the locksmith, came a few minutes later, it seemed only hospitable to ask them if they wouldn't like a second cup of coffee before starting to work. At this point the furnaceman, Mr. Thurple, arrived in the painter's automobile (I didn't quite catch the painter's name, but I think it was Schnee; at any rate, I called him Schnee and he seemed quite pleased), and so our little coffee party was now six, including the host, which just filled the breakfast table nicely.

"Do you take cream in your coffee, Mr. Margotson?" I asked. Mr. Margotson and Mr. Rallif having been the first to arrive, it seemed to me that they should be served first.

"It's strange that you should have asked me that," replied Mr. Margotson, "for I was saying to Mrs. Margotson at breakfast only this morning, 'I see in the paper where a man says that cream *and* sugar together in coffee set up a poison which sooner or later results in a toxæmia!'"

"Don't you think," put in Mr. Thurple, helping himself to cream and sugar, "that we are, as a nation, becoming a little too self-conscious about what we eat and drink? As a nation, I mean."

Mr. Schnee, or whatever his name was, laughed a low, tinkling laugh. This, although Mr. Schnee said nothing, somehow broke the ice and we all laughed. I had never seen five more congenial and delightful men together at one table (six, if you want to count me; I couldn't very well have said it of myself). As soon as we all had our coffee cups well poised, the conversation became general and drifted from dietetics to religion and then quickly back to dietetics again. When Mr. Ramm, the plumber (true to the jokes in the funny papers, the last to arrive), came bursting in he found us deep in a discussion of whether or not ransom should be paid in kidnaping cases.

"The late Mr. Ramm!" taunted Mr. Thurple, the furnaceman, who had already established himself as the clown of the crowd by having seven cups of coffee. At which sally Mr. Schnee again laughed his low, tinkling laugh and set us all off again. As soon as Mr. Ramm had recovered from his embarrassment at being the butt of Mr. Thurple's joke, I set the round of day's activities in motion.

"How many here play badminton?" I asked, springing to my feet.

"I," "I," and "I," came with a will from three hearty throats, and Messrs. Margotson, Rallif, and Thurple had their coats off and their sleeves rolled up as an earnest of their intentions.

"Take me, I like backgammon," said Mr. Ramm.

"You're my man then," said Mr. Shrank. "I am the

backgammon king of Locksmiths' Row." It looked for a minute as if we were in for a rather nasty argument, but Mr. Schnee's low, musical laugh came again to the rescue, and the party was on. The room which had been full of men only a minute before was now emptied in a trice, some rushing pell-mell to the badminton court and some to the backgammon room.

Luncheon was a gay affair, with favors for those who had won at their various games and speeches of acceptance which convulsed even the low-laughing Mr. Schnee.

"I am sorry, gentlemen," I said, in part, when it came my turn, "that I have got you all here to do certain jobs to which you are severally suited by training and study, for I find that I have not the money to pay you with, even if you were to carry out your commissions. But what there is of good cheer and good fellowship in this house is yours, and we are all going to make the most of it while it lasts."

That was a month and a half ago and they are all still living with me. We are the best of friends and still the small boys at heart that we always were. The house is in much worse condition than it was before; but, as it turned out that they all had more money than I, I am not worrying. They have each promised to buy a story from me as soon as I can get around to writing it.

*A*tom *B*oy!

With all that I have to do, it seems a little too bad that I should have to keep worrying about the constitution of the atom. One day Sir Arthur Reeves Reeves-Arthur comes out and says that the atom is made up of electrons and protons. The following week Dr. Hjalmar Rensnessen reads a paper before the Royal Society of Locomotive Engineers and says that the atom is composed of little pieces of old pocket lint. The hell with both of them! I can't be bothered.

There is one feature of these researches, however, which holds my attention for almost a quarter of a second. Someone (his name slips my mind right now, but I have it in my files in case you ever should want it) has figured out that, if we could utilize the energy in an atom, we would never have to do any more work ourselves. Now, *there's* a scientist! *There's* the boy for me! He doesn't say what we are going to nibble on when we go out to the ice box to get a cold snack before going to bed, or what strange medium of exchange we are going to use to buy it with, since none of us are working, but he does say that we won't be working, and that is the main thing. The eating will take care of itself. We can eat each other. And I already have a list of twenty people whom I *don't* want to eat.

As I understand it (which I don't), each atom has a so-called "nucleus" at its center, like that cute little old Daddy Worm in the center of a chestnut. This part I have decided not to think about.

But when you consider that each atom is only a hundred-millionths of an inch across (that would be even smaller than the piece of lobster in a lobster and shrimp Newburgh) and that its nucleus is only about ten-thousandths of this diameter, you will not only see how small a nucleus is but you will also go a little crazy. In fact, in just writing these figures down on paper I have whipped myself into such a state that I have got the typewriter ribbon all tangled up in my fingers and am going to have to drop everything and bathe my temples.

So what?

So if we can split an atom (I am using the slang of Prof. E. N. daC. Andrade in the London Observer) and *then* can split the nucleus, we are going to find a lot of little things called "protons" and "electrons," and you can imagine how small they are going to be. It is absurd. The protons are positive and the electrons are negative, and, of the two, I am sure that the electrons are nicer. I hate a positive proton They think they know everything. It is "This is so" and "That is so," until you want to smack them in the face. With the world in the state it is in today, nobody can be as positive as all that.

Now Prof. E. N. daC. Andrade (until I know what the "daC." in the professor's name stands for, I shall be tossing and turning all night) suggests that, in order to break up these atoms and nuclei (hot dickity), we shall have to use some very powerful projectile to smash into them at a tremendous rate of speed. Just who is going to pick up what is left after this projectile has hit the atom and make the pieces look like anything at all, is something I, personally, am not going to worry about.

In fact, I have lost a great deal of interest in the whole subject since starting to write this article, and I am sure that you have, too, my great big Audience of Rodeo Land. Suppose we let the whole matter drop for a while and just give ourselves over to fun and frolic?

It seems there were three Irishmen, whom we will call three Hungarians because that was not their name. Well, these three chaps were walking along the street when one of them turned to the other two (he being on the outside) and said: "Stop your pushing!" You can imagine the hubbub which resulted from this remark. Fists flew like hot cakes and in no time at all, the only one left was the man who had made the original remark, the other two having been Scotsmen, and, being Scotsmen, had saved their strength for six per cent. This more or less makes a bum out of the original story which, if you will consult your notes, was to have been about three Irishmen. It just seems as if *nothing* held together these days. I think there was even more to the story than the tantalizing bit I have given you, but it is too late now. We are back again on the atom.

We now come to the fascinating part of our paper. According to Professor You-Know, "the gun which fires the projectiles is the nucleus of atoms of radioactive substances, such as the element called 'Radium C'; the projectiles are the so-called 'alpha' particles (*Editor's Note: 'So-called' by whom?*), which are themselves small nuclei, and consist of four protons and two electrons welded together."

This makes it all a little clearer. All that we have to do in order to split an atom is to go to the nearest druggist and ask him for a small package of Radium C. Radium A and Radium B are for the big boys and can be had only by presenting an order from the Headmaster.

I am not kidding when I tell you that Dr. Ernest Rutherford has succeeded in directing a stream of alpha particles from radioactive substances on to certain light elements and has knocked several representative atoms into a cocked hat. The cocked hat has then been taken, covered with an American flag, and, when uncovered, has been found to contain an old rabbit and sixty yards of red tissue paper. The applause which greeted this trick of Dr. Rutherford's was nothing short of deafening.

"It has long been my ambition" (it is Dr. Rutherford speaking) "to have available a copious supply of atoms and electrons which have an individual energy far transcending that of the alpha and beta particles from radioactive bodies."

The applause which greeted this trick was nothing short of deafening.

Now here is where the surprise comes in! A few of us are getting together, unbeknownst to Dr. Rutherford, of whom we are very fond, and are going to chip in and help him fulfill this ambition of his. We are going to get him a whole case of the atoms and electrons that he has been longing for and are going around to his laboratory some day and leave them on his doorstep, with a note reading: "Dear Doc: A little bird told us that you wanted some of these. Don't open them until your birthday. Then go to it, and *split those atoms!*"

Perhaps this is making a great deal of to-do about nothing. But if somebody thinks that he can fix it so that none of us will ever have to work again, I think that we ought to help him. It probably will come too late to be of much use to us of the present generation, but, from the looks of things now, our children are going to have to work awfully hard unless something like this comes along to save them. In the meantime, I am more or less resting on my oars and waiting. It may come sooner than we think.

$\mathcal{W}$hat $\mathcal{A}$bout Business?

I HAVE been asked (by a couple of small boys and a wire-haired fox terrier) to summarize briefly my views on the Business and Financial Outlook for 1931. I would have done this long ago, together with the other financial and business experts, but I wanted first to wait and see if there really was going to be a 1931 or not.

Just because a year has started off with a January and February is no sign that it is going to continue on indefinitely through the rest of the months.

But, as it looks now, we are in for a year which will be known as 1931. Just what else it will be known as remains to be seen, but I have got a good name all worked up for it if it turns out to be like 1930. However, I am not here to talk dirty. I am here to outline the economic forces and currents which have contributed to the present business and financial situation and to predict their course during the year which is now well on its way. In doing this I will stick pretty closely to the formula followed by the 2,300,000 experts who have already preceded me in this prognostication. I haven't read them all, but I got a fairly close idea of what they were driving at.

As I understand it (which is just about *that* much—or perhaps even *that* much), there are several causes which are responsible for the depression of 1930 and which I will list in the order of their legibility on my note pad:

Overproduction, a breakdown in artificial control over commodity prices, maladjustments in gold distribution, overproduction, faulty ignition, overproduction, deflation, subnormal thyroid secretion (or "Platt's Disease"), too much vermouth, deflation, excess of charts with black lines, excess of charts with red lines, and overproduction. Let us take these up, one by one, and then drop dead.

First, overproduction. In 1925 (which brings us down to 1927) we exported this commodity to the extent of twenty-four billion bushels, obviously too much. In 1929 this had been increased by sixty-eight bushels, or one bushel for each of the sixty-eight states in the Union. This increase, together with a simultaneous *decrease* in deflation, or consumer resistance, brought about a situation in which the world's markets found themselves faced with what amounted to, in round numbers, a pretty pickle.

Thus we see that this shortsighted policy of increasing production and, at the same time, decreasing inflation (or "Platt's Disease") brought on a crisis in distribution (or deflation) which naturally led to speculation in "shorts" (lobsters under six inches in length which are supposed, according to the Law, to be thrown back when caught. "Shorts," however, have much sweeter meat than the larger lobsters and it is often a great temptation to cheat just a teeny-weeny bit and take them home. They are delicious when served with melted butter).

The fall in silver which accompanied this ridiculous state of affairs naturally cut the purchasing power of the Far East, except in those countries where lozenges are used as legal tender. And with the purchasing power of the Far East diminished, and the importation of old rugs and punk from the Far East increasing, it is little wonder that people got so that they didn't know whether they were coming or going. Often they were doing both.

I am afraid that I can't be of much help to this discussion in the matter of gold and silver supply. I never quite caught on to what the hell it was all about.

We hear that there is a shortage of gold or an oversupply

of gold; that France has all the gold or that the United States has all the gold. What gold? I don't mean to insinuate anything, but how did France *get* all this gold if she shouldn't have it? Where did she get it from? And what does she do with it when she gets it? And who cares, so long as there are plenty of good, crisp bank notes in circulation?

Give me a bank note every time. Then you aren't so likely to give it away under the impression that it is a lucky penny. I once gave a neighbor's little boy a lucky penny which was so lucky that he got five dollars for it at the bank. The whole system is rotten to the core.

But to return to our business forecast. (If you don't want to return, there are books and magazines on the table in the anteroom, and we will be right out in a few minutes.) I look

It is often a great temptation to cheat just a teeny-weeny bit and take them home.

for the following changes in our economic system which should radically alter conditions for the better:

(1) There will be, if I have anything to say about it, a remedy for overproduction in the marked decrease in the manufacture of greeting cards, shirts that go on over the head, auto busses, gin-and-orange-juice cocktails, war books, washroom boys, seed rolls, tops to toothpaste tubes, art furniture, automatic elevators, paper matches. (I am rather sorry now that I began this list. There are so many things, and they are so difficult to remember.)

(2) In 1931 I look for a decided betterment in the relation of bond to stock yields. That is, of stock to bond yields. The ratio, as near as I can make it out without my glasses, is 4.70% as compared to 5.76%. (These figures are as of July, 1930, and what a hot month *that* was! I was at the seashore, and never got out of my bathing suit once, except to go in bathing.) Now this ratio, together with the increase in deflation and the decrease in inflation which must inevitably come about with the unfortunate and unpleasant distribution of gold which exists at the present moment (mentioning no names, but it begins with "F" and is a country noted for its dancing and light wines), will tend to break down the artificial control of commodity prices and possibly restore public confidence to a point where people will dare to go out into the street and perhaps walk one block under police escort.

(3) Money will be less scarce. By this I do not mean that you and I will have *more* money, or that it will be any less scarce when you look inside your wallet when the dinner check comes. There seems to be another kind of money that the banks handle. It is "plentiful," or it is "scarce," or it is "cheap," or it is "high."

Personally, I have never been able to get hold of any cheap money. If I want five dollars, it always costs me five dollars to get it, or, at any rate, a check for five dollars made out to "Cash" (which may, or may not, be the same thing). I never could figure out whether "cheap" money meant that a five-dollar bill cost only four dollars and sixty cents to buy, or that it was in bad condition, with torn edges and little strings hanging from it so that it *looked* cheap. At any rate, whatever "cheap" money means to bankers, five dollars is always five dollars to me. And a hundred dollars is a godsend.

However, in a forecast of this sort, one must always say that money will be less scarce—so here goes: Money will be less scarce.

(4) Now about wheat. Wheat seems to have a lot to do with world conditions, although with so many people trying to reduce weight, I should think that it would be less important now than it was in 1900. Here again, like the money the banks use, the wheat referred to in the quotations must be another kind of wheat than that which goes into those delicious hot rolls we have at home. (Did you ever try dunking hot rolls in maple sirup? When you get down to the crisp brown part it just doesn't seem as if you could bear it.) The wheat we hear about in the financial quotations never comes in bundles of less than a million bushels, which, frankly, sounds a little unappetizing. When you get up into figures like that with just plain wheat, you run the risk of just sounding silly.

In fact, I am not sure that the whole financial and business structure on which our system is founded is not silly, with its billions of bushels and billions of gold bars and nothing to show for it.

I am working on a plan now whereby we scrap the whole thing and begin all over again, with a checking account for ten thousand dollars in my name in some good bank. With a head start like that I ought to be able to get my own affairs cleaned up, and with my own affairs cleaned up I am sure that world affairs would look a lot rosier.

$\mathcal{L}$aughter
and $\mathcal{A}$pplause

WHEN radio first came into general use (I can remember the first electric light, too—or, rather, the first electric light we ever had in our house. It had probably been done somewhere else before), it looked for a while as if broadcasting was going to put a stop to the old-fashioned scarf dance which public speakers had been indulging in under the head of public speaking. When a speaker could face his audience and flash those fiery black eyes or shake those wavy locks and get that business-like sex appeal into play, it didn't make much difference what his speech consisted of. He could be saying "Hill-dill-come-over-the-hill-or-else-I'll-catch-you-standing-still" and his audience wouldn't know the difference. A great many elections were won in this manner.

It certainly seemed that radio would put a stop to all this. When a man gets up in front of a microphone it doesn't make any difference whether he has got great, big, brown eyes or no eyes at all. Unless he cares what the musicians think, he doesn't even have to shave. But his talk has got to be worth listening to or there is going to be a general turning of dials all over the civilized world, leaving him hanging in the middle of a four-syllable word. Or, at least, that is what we all hoped would be the result. I am not so sure now.

A while ago I listened in on a speech being made in London by George Bernard Shaw, who is a clever guy, too. He was introducing Professor Einstein at some banquet or something—possibly a handout for the unemployed. I couldn't hear what Professor Einstein said, because just at that time the nest of field mice which live in my radio set began gnawing their way out, getting a couple of beavers to help them. But I did hear Mr. Shaw, and I heard the effect he was having on his audience. There is an old superstition that the English are slow at getting a joke, but I want to tell you that the Englishmen at that banquet were in a laughing mood which bordered on nervous hysteria. They were laughing at commas. All Mr. Shaw had to do was to say, "And, furthermore—" and the house came down. Of all the push-over audiences I have ever heard, they had the least gag resistance.

What they would have done if they had heard a *real* gag is rather terrifying to think about. Blood vessels would have been bursting like toy balloons and the salvage of collar buttons and dress ties which would have flown to the floor might easily have filled twelve baskets.

I thought at first that something (more than usual) was wrong with my radio, and that I wasn't getting the last few words of the witty sallies which were being received with such a din. But the next day the papers carried the Shaw speech verbatim, and I found to my horror that I had heard every word. Here is a sample of what set London by the ears that night, with my own italics to indicate its effect on the listeners:

Mr. Shaw: "Ladies and gentlemen (*laughter*): When my friend Mr. Wells asked me to take this duty, I could not help wondering whether he realized the honor he was conferring upon me (*prolonged laughter*), and whether I was able to discharge it adequately. (*Three minutes of hysteria.*) I felt I could only do my best. (*Crashing applause.*) Here in London we are still a great factor, but no doubt presently that will be transferred to the United States. (*The first real gag, throwing the place into pandemonium.*) . . . We have a string of great financiers, great diplomats, and even occasionally an author (*intermission while half a dozen listeners with weak hearts are carried out*), and we make pictures as we talk." (*Complete collapse of roof, as the diners beat each other in a frenzy.*)

*I did hear Mr. Shaw, and I heard the effect he was having on his audience.
They were laughing at commas.*

This, then, was the opening of Mr. Shaw's speech, and I
had, with my own ears, heard what it was doing to the hand-
picked audience in front of him. There were two possible
explanations: first, that it was over my head; and, second,
that the entire London group had been up in Room 211
before the banquet commenced and were cockeyed drunk.

I like a laugh as well as anyone, and I am accustomed to
laugh loudly at Mr. Shaw's plays, occasionally because I am
amused, but more often because by laughing at Mr. Shaw's
plays one lets the rest of the audience know that one is on
the inside and gets the subtler meanings. But as I listened
to the speech of the great man on this occasion, I felt that

what few giggles I might be able to throw out would be so inadequate in the face of what was going on in London that I had much better just listen quietly and mind my own business.

Now this sound effect of an audience in a fever heat of enthusiasm is what is going to save radio speakers. And it has given rise to an entirely new trade, the professional Applause-Donor or Audience-Sitter. They sit in the radio studio —at so much a sit—and on signal from a director, laugh, sob, or beat their hands together. If a really good effect is desired they can be induced to ring cowbells and twirl policemen's rattles. It is barely possible that Mr. Shaw had a couple of hundred of these at work for him.

I once made a speech over the radio (there must have been a ship sinking at sea that night, for I never could find anyone who heard it) and, when I entered the studio, I was surprised to see about fifteen people of assorted ages and get-ups sitting very grimly over against the wall. I thought at first that they constituted some choir or team of Swiss bell ringers who were going to follow me on the program, but the announcer told me that they were my audience and that, whenever he gave the signal, they would burst into laughter and applause so that my larger audience in radioland would think that they were listening in on a wow. All that this did was to make me nervous. Furthermore, I could feel that my professional laughers had taken an immediate and instinctive dislike to me.

I began on my speech, after a few salvos of applause from the benches, and for the first couple of times, on signal from the overseer, got a pretty fair assortment of laughs. But as the gags kept getting thinner and thinner I detected a feeling of mutiny stirring through the ranks of my professional audience, and the director had harder and harder work to get anything resembling a genuine-sounding laugh out of his crew.

He was furious, but, owing to the necessity for silence, was unable to bawl them out or even say, "Come on now, louder!" At last the revolt broke and, just as he had given the signal for a round of laughter and applause, three of the workers got up and tiptoed from the room, automatically resigning from their jobs as they went. Even my paid audience was walking out on me. They were followed by half a dozen others, who evidently felt that, money or no money, there was such a thing as personal pride, even in their profession. By the time I had finished there was only one of the claque left, and she was asleep.

The announcer told me, when we got outside, that such a thing had never happened before, and that the company would start suit against the mutineers the next day, as they were all under contract. He added that it might be better if I left the building by the back entrance, where he would have a cab waiting for me to duck into. I promised that the next time I made a radio speech I would bring my own applause-donors, relatives of mine, if possible, but he said that we would discuss that when the time came.

So whenever you hear a speech over the air which seems to be knocking the audience cold, you needn't feel that it is your fault if you don't like it yourself. Just picture a row of disgruntled workers sitting against the wall of the studio, muttering under their breaths.

It doesn't seem possible that Mr. Shaw could have hired so many "supers" as there seemed to have been at his London dinner, but the unemployment situation in London is much worse than it is here and you can probably get people to do anything for money. I'd like to get about a dozen of them over here for my next radio appearance. I'd be a riot.

_H_ow

the _D_oggie _G_oes

A WELL known goldfish once referred to someone as having
no more privacy than Irvin Cobb, but I would like to bet
that the most publicly mauled and openly examined human
being in the country today is the child of three. A child of
three cannot raise its chubby fist to its mouth to remove a
piece of carpet which it is through eating, without being made
the subject of a psychological seminar of child-welfare experts, and written up, along with five hundred other children
of three who have put their hands to their mouths for the
same reason, in a paper entitled: The Ratio of Mouth-
Thumbing in Children of Sub-School Age in Its Relation to
Carpet-Eating.

Now they have begun to examine children to see why
they say "I won't!" when Mummy asks them to tell nice
Mrs. Kalbfleisch what the mooley-cow says. Up until now
when a child has said "I won't!" to such a demand it has
seemed merely that it was the only possible reply to make.
Just why a person, simply because he is only two years old,
should feel any obligation to tell Mrs. Kalbfleisch what the
mooley-cow says, is a mystery which any open-minded observer has difficulty in fathoming.

Who wouldn't say "I won't!" and pretty sharply, too, if
asked to say "Moo-oo!" to Mrs. Kalbfleisch? Is there anything strange in a child's making the same reply?

But the child-welfare people seem to think that the matter

has to be gone into. They took children ranging in age from eighteen to forty-eight months (who probably, in the first place, were pretty sore at being dragged in from the sand pile and old fish just to answer a lot of questions) and subjected them, according to the report, to "2,352 items of a verbal nature and 2,057 requiring some degree of physical reaction." That must have taken the best part of an afternoon and I guess that along about four thirty there must have been quite a bit of snarling and sulking going on, even among the examiners. I know, if I had been on the grille, what *one* of my 2,057 physical reactions would have been and it would have landed squarely between somebody's eyes.

"In each case," continues the report, "the child's resistance to the test was carefully recorded as one of the four criteria. Some children simply ignored the question." (Those children will go far. They are the white hopes of the future generation.) "Others verbally resisted with a shrill but determined 'I won't tell you!'" (The more excitable type, on the right track, but using up too much nervous energy in making their point. They should be told to watch the ones who simply ignored the questions and pattern after them.) "A third group resisted physically by running from the room or scampering into a corner." (This would have been my own personal reaction as a child, or even now for that matter, and it is a trait which has got me nowhere, as you have to come back sooner or later and there they are with the question again.) "Still others indicated inability to answer by whining 'I can't' or 'I don't know.'" (This was probably a lie on the part of the children, but it is a pretty good way out. You get the reputation for being stupid, but after a while you are let alone. I would say that the best methods were the first and the last, either ignoring the thing entirely or saying "I don't know." If you say "I won't" or scamper into a corner it just eggs the examiners on.)

The tests included the fitting of geometrical figures into a special form board ("I can't" would be my answer right now); attaching limbs to the body of a manikin; putting square and round pegs into a perforated board; responding to such commands as "Stand on your left foot" or "Cross your feet" (to be ignored unless the examiner added "please"); recognizing one's self in a mirror (a great deal of fun could be had with the examiner by saying "I never saw this person before in my life," and sticking to it); fitting a nest of cubes together (Oh, hell! You might as well do that one for them!); and answering "What does a doggie say?" and "What mews?" To the question "What mews?" you could kid along and say you haven't seen a mewspaper that day, adding that no mews is good mews. This would confuse the examiner and perhaps make him discouraged enough to go home.

Such questions as "What does the doggie say?" and "How does the mooley-cow go?" come in a group by themselves. In the first place, any self-respecting child should insist that the question be rephrased, using "dog" instead of "doggie" and "cow" instead of "mooley-cow." This is only simple justice. Then, if any answer is to be given at all (and I recommend against it), it should be delivered with considerable

scorn as follows: "The dog doesn't *say* anything. It barks, if that is what you mean."

Presumably the child, while it is at the business of learning to talk, is supposed to be learning the kind of talk it will have some use for in after years, otherwise it would be taught only to make gargling noises in its throat and phrases like "Glub-glub." Now the chances are very small of its wanting ever to say "Bow-wow" in ordinary conversation unless it is going to give imitations when it grows up or else is planning to drink heavily. So why make it say "Bow-wow" in answer to the dog question, especially as that isn't what a dog says anyway? No child should allow itself to be made a fool of like that.

I personally was made to see the error of this system by a very small child who took matters into his own hands and made a fool out of me even before I had begun to do it for myself. When I would ask him what the dog said, he would reply "Moo-oo," and when I persisted, he would change it to "Toot-toot" and "Tick-tick."

At first I thought that I had a cretin on my hands and got to brooding over it. Then one day, when I had got "Bow-wow" as an answer to what the "choo-choo train" said, I detected a slight twinkle, not unmixed with scorn, in the child's eye, and as he walked off, a trifle unsteadily, I was sure that I heard a hoarse guttural laugh, not unlike what the goat says. So I stopped asking him to imitate animals and machines and took him to ball games instead. It has since transpired that he knew what he was doing and was planning to start throwing things at me if I had gone on much longer.

I *will* say this for the Child Development Institute, however. The conclusions which they made from their investigations were that the children had been asked to do so many things during the day, usually prefaced with "Come on, Junior. Won't you, please?" or told to "say please" or "say thank you," that they just simply got so damned sick of the whole silly mess that they refused to do anything. Or, in the words of the report, "a total of 161 resistances were noted. . . . The specific question, 'What is your name?' was resisted nine times out of a hundred, probably because the child's previous experience in being asked his name on each and every occasion by well meaning adults has already conditioned him negatively to this question."

Although the wording of the foregoing is a bit formal, it is very sensible. It says "conditioned him negatively" instead of "pretty damned sick of it," but the meaning is the same. Sometime I would like to get a group of children to ask a lot of silly questions of one grown-up at a time, such as "What is your name?" and "How does the bossy go?" and see just how long it would be before the grown-ups were down on the floor kicking and screaming, or, along with me, scampering into a corner. Then perhaps we would all begin at scratch again and live and let live.

*T*he
*R*ailroad *P*roblem

I UNDERSTAND that there is a big plan on foot to consolidate the railways of this country into four large systems. This doesn't interest me much, as I walk almost everywhere I go. (I discovered that I was putting on quite a bit of weight and was told that walking was fine for that sort of thing, but, since making the resolution to walk everywhere I go, I find that I just don't *go* anywhere. As a result, I have gained six pounds and never felt better in my life.)

However, there must be people who use the railroads or they wouldn't keep blowing those whistles all the time. And it is in behalf of these people that I would like to make a few suggestions to the new consolidated systems, suggestions based on my experiences when I used to be a traveler myself. I jotted down notes of them at the time, but notes made on a moving train are not always very legible the next day, and I am afraid that I shall have to guess at most of them (especially those written with the pen in the club car) and rely on my memory for the rest.

What I want to know is—what are they going to do about the heating systems? In the new arrangement, something very drastic has got to be done about running those steam pipes under my individual berth. I have tried every berth from Lower One to Upper Fourteen on every line in the country except the Montour and the Detroit, Toledo, & Ironton, and in every damned one of them I was the central point for the heating system of the whole train.

It wouldn't be so bad if, when I had finally accommodated myself to lying beside a steam pipe by throwing off all the flannel pads which serve as blankets and going to sleep like Diana at the Bath (oh, well, not *exactly* like Diana but near enough for the purpose of *this* story), they didn't then run ammonia through that very pipe and set up a refrigerating system along about four in the morning. They might at least make up their minds as to whether they want to roast or freeze me. It's this constant vacillating that upsets me.

Now in this new system of railroads, while they are deciding so many questions, they might as well decide about me. I will be a good sport about it, whatever they say. But I *do* want to know what the plan is. Is it to roast or freeze Benchley? Then I can make my own plans accordingly.

And while they are at it, they might work up some system of instruction which would eliminate new engineers taking their driving lessons on night runs. As I have figured it out, this is the way the thing is worked now:

The regular engineer takes the train until about three in the morning. Then the new man gets aboard and is shown the throttles and is instructed about how to put on his overalls and gloves. If the system is working well, this is the first time the new man has ever been near an engine in his life. A porter then comes rushing up from back in the train and announces: "O.K., boys! Benchley is asleep! Let-er ride!"

At this point the instructor tells the new man to start her up easy. The man, with that same enthusiasm which makes a beginner in automobile driving stall the engine right off the bat, starts "her" up as if he were trying to take off in a helicopter and rise right up off the ground. The result is that all the cars in the train follow for the distance of one foot and then crash together, forming one composite car.

"No, no, no, Joe!" shouts the instructor, laughing. "Take her easy! Let her in slowly. Look, let me show you!" So he does it, and the cars unscramble themselves and stand trembling, waiting for the next crash. I myself have, by this time, sat bolt upright in my berth in spite of a broken collar bone. It is not until I have snuggled down again that the

The occupant of Lower Two finds himself in Lower Fourteen.

novice up in the cab tries his hand again. This time he is a little better and gets the train ahead about ten feet before he forgets what to do next, grows panicky, and jams on his emergency. I venture to say that, on his second try, he sends me a good four inches into the headboard of the berth.

"At-a-boy, Joe!" encourages his mentor. "You'll learn in no time. Now, just give her one more bang and then I'll take it over. You've had enough for one night."

So Joe has one more, or maybe two more bangs and then goes back to take his first lesson in coupling and uncoupling. This is no small job to undertake for the first time in the dark, and he does awfully well under the circumstances. All that he does is to drive the Anastasia into the Bellerophon so far that the occupant of Lower Two in the first-named car finds himself in bed with the occupant of Lower Fourteen in the second. Not bad for a starter, Joe. You'll be a brakeman *and* an engineer before you know it. (I take it for granted that it is the same pupil who is driving the engine and coupling the cars. There couldn't be *two* men like that on one train.)

Now, if there can be no way devised under the new system to have these new boys try out their lessons in some school in the yards, using dummy trains instead of real ones full of real passengers, then the least that the roads can do is to have the lesson hour come during the day when people are sitting upright and have a little resistance power. When these crashes come in the daytime (and they do, they do) you can at least brace yourself and look out of the window to see whether or not the train has landed in the branches of a tree. The new railroad systems should recognize that there is a time for work and a time for play and that four A.M. is *not* the time for romping among the younger engineers.

There are one or two other points which ought to be brought out in this little petition, points which the roads would do well to take to heart if steam travel is ever to supplant flying as a mode of transportation.

(1) Those two men who shout under my window whenever a train comes to a halt in a station during the night. I have heard what they have to say, and it really isn't worth shouting. One of them is named Mac, in case the officials want to go into this thing any further.

(2) The piling up of bags in the vestibule by the porters on day trains. In the old days we used to carry our bags out ourselves, and, irksome as it was, we at least got out of the train. As it is today, the train has been in the station a good half hour before the porter has dug into the mountain of suitcases in the vestibule so that it is low enough for a man on a burro to climb over it. The roads should either add this half hour to their running time on the time-tables (Ar. N.Y. 4:30. Disembark N.Y. 4:55) or else cut a hole in the roof to let out those passengers who have other connections to make.

(3) The polish used by porters in shining shoes. This should either be made of *real* gum so that it will attract articles of value, like coins and buttons, or of real polish so that the shoes will shine. As it is, the shoes neither shine nor are they sticky enough to attract anything more tangible than dust and fluff.

Here again it is a case in which the roads must make up their mind. Before they can amalgamate they must make up their mind on a lot of things. I have already made up mine.

*A H*istory

of *P*laying *C*ards

NOT many of you little rascals who employ playing cards
for your own diversion or for the diversion of your funds
know how playing cards were first used. And I venture to say
that not many of you care. So here we are, off on a voyage of
exploration into the History of the Playing Card, or Where
Did All That Money Go Last Week?

The oldest existing playing cards, aside from those which
I keep in the back of my desk for Canfield, are in the
Staatliches Museum in Berlin and are Chinese. Don't ask
me how Chinese playing cards got into Berlin. Do I know
everything? Suffice it to say that they are a thousand years
old, which gives them perhaps twelve or fifteen years on my
Canfield pack. My Canfield pack, however, has more thumb
marks.

These thousand-year-old Chinese cards would be practically no good for anyone today who wanted to sit down for a
good game of rummy. What corresponds to our ace (I am
told there is such a card in our pack—I have never seen one
myself except once when drawing to a 5–9 straight) is a handful of scorpions, and the king and queen are not like our
kings and queens but more like dragons with beards and
headdresses. A gentleman who had been playing bridge with
a ginger-ale highball at his elbow for two hours would never
get around to bidding if he found one of those kings or
queens in his hand. It would undermine his confidence in
himself.

Authorities differ on the point of the invention of playing cards. Some say that it was the Egyptians, some the Arabs, while others maintain that it was part of an old Phœnician torture system by which a victim was handed thirteen cards and made to lay them down, one by one, in the proper sequence, the proper sequence being known only to an inquisitor known as the partner. If the cards were not laid down in the sequence prescribed by the inquisitor, the victim was strung up by the thumbs and glared at until he was dead of mortification. I rather incline to this last theory of the origin of the playing card. But that may be because I am bitter.

Fig. 1   Fig. 2

There is also a theory that playing cards and chess were originally the same game. This might very well be, although I don't see where the card players would get the chance to sleep that chess players do. A good chess player can tear off anywhere from forty to sixty-five winks a move, if he is clever at it and hides his eyes with his hand, but a card player has at least got to sit up straight and do *something*. It may not be the thing to do, but he has got to do something.

I have often wished, as a matter of fact, that bridge plays could be handled in the same way as chess moves, for if I were given time and a good excuse for covering my face, I could do an awful lot better at bridge than I do. If, when my partner led out with a four of clubs, I could cup my hand over my brow and ponder, let us say for two minutes and a half, I might figure out what the hell it was she meant by her lead.

Whether or not chessmen and playing cards were once all a part of the same big game, the fact remains that a lot of the old playing cards look as if they belonged to some other game than bridge or poker.

For example, take the card which is shown in Fig. 1—the one involving the services of what seems to be an old ant-eater and three nasturtiums. I can't quite figure out what the game would be which could possibly make it desirable to draw one of these. Perhaps three of such cards as this and two of the kind showing a crane and some lily pads would be as good as a full house—but I doubt it. I can't imagine thrilling to a draw which resulted in two such cards as that shown in Fig. 2, in which a gentleman seems to be slapping down cockroaches. I would much rather see a simple little four spot (if I already held a five, six, seven, and eight) than any number of political cartoons like those in Fig. 3, showing the Duke of Marlborough setting Queen Anne on fire.

In the old days cards were apparently designed to fill in those intervals in a game during which the player was bored with looking at his partner (I can understand that all right) and just wanted to while away the time by looking at pictures.

Even when they got to putting pictures that one can understand on playing cards—kings, queens, jacks, etc.—it was a long time before they made them look like anything at all. If you will take a look at the queen shown in playing card number 4 you will see that she looks so much like a jack that there is no fun in it. Furthermore, she has a very unpleasant expression on her face and I'll bet that she sings soprano without being asked. If I were to draw her, together with a jack, ten, nine, and three (as I *would*, you may be sure), I

Fig. 3   Fig. 4

would discard both her and the three in the wild hope of filling to both ends rather than hold a hand with such an unpleasant-looking old girl in it. Anyway, I would probably think that she was a jack and keep the two for a possible five of a kind. (I don't play poker very well.)

My theory about the origin of the people shown on playing cards is this—

Oh, well, if you don't care, I certainly don't.

It has always seemed to me that the king and queen in an ordinary pack were based on real characters in history, a king and a queen who never got along very well together and wanted to separate. If the king saw the queen coming (in *my* hand, at any rate), he ducked up an alley and said to the jack: "Listen, son, you go that way and I'll go this, and I'll meet you when the game is over at Tony's. Don't let the Old Lady get in touch with you. She'll only make trouble." So the king goes one way and the jack goes another, and I am stuck with the queen and an eight-four-two, with (in case of bridge) a six spot of some other suit, and others to match.

This, according to my theory, is the real history of the characters in our playing cards. They were the most unhappy royal family in any of the old-time chronicles, and somebody thought that it would be a good idea to put them on playing cards just to torture me personally. I don't know about the early cards, with the duck shooters and anteater stalkers on them. But I venture to say that if I were playing the game, they would all be in the conspiracy, too. For this I have a very simple solution: I stick to Canfield where a man has at least a fighting chance to cheat.

The Five

(or Maybe Six)

Year Plan

IF I hear any more about this five-year-plan business I am going to start one myself. Russia has been working on hers for a couple of years now, and England is thinking of starting one, and what Russia and England can do, I can do. All that is necessary is for me to find out just what a five-year-plan is.

As I understand it, you take five years to start all over again. You throw out all your old systems, clean out the rubbers in the hall closet, give to the Salvation Army all those old bundles of the National Geographic you have been saving, and tell your creditors to wait for five years and that they will be surprised to see how well you pay. It sounds like a good plan to me. I haven't asked my butcher about it yet.

When a nation goes in for a five-year plan it reorganizes everything, eliminates competition, buys everything on a large scale, sells everything in amalgamations, and, in general, acts up big. I can't do that, because I shall be working alone and on my own, but I *can* reorganize, and I figure that it will take me about five years to do the thing right. Let's say six and be on the safe side.

In the first place, my whole financial system has got to be gone over. It is in such bad shape now that it can hardly be called a system. In fact, I don't think that it can even be called financial. It is more of a carnival. I shall have to go through all those old checkbook stubs and throw them out, for, under my present method of keeping books, there was no need of saving them, anyway. You see, it has been quite some time since I subtracted the amounts of checks drawn from what I smilingly call the "balance." In fact, there are often great stretches of time when I don't even enter the amounts at all. This latter irregularity is due to a habit of making out checks on blank forms supplied by hotels and restaurants, on which even the name of the bank has to be filled in, to say nothing of the number of the check and its amount. I like to make these out, because I print rather well and it is a great satisfaction to letter in the name of my bank in neat capitals exactly in the middle of the space provided for that purpose. I have sometimes made out a blank check just for the satisfaction of seeing "BANKERS' TRUST CO., 57th St. Branch" come out in such typographical perfection from the point of my pen. I am sure that it is a satisfaction to the bank, too. They often speak of it. What they object to is the amount which I fill in below. It seems too bad, they say, to have such a neat-looking check so unnegotiable. All of this will be changed under my five-year plan, for I intend not only to give up making out blank checks, but to enter and subtract those which I do make out. I cannot guarantee to subtract them correctly, for I am not a superman and can do only one thing at a time, but I will at least get the figures down on paper. The bank can handle the rest, and I am sure that they will. That is what they pay men to do, and they have never failed me yet.

Which brings us to the second part of my new economic reorganization—production. Some way has got to be found to turn out more work. One solution would be, I suppose, to do more work, but that seems a little drastic. If Russia and England can combine all their forces to speed up production, I ought to be able to combine with somebody to speed up mine without making a slave of myself as well. If I could get a dozen or so fellows who are in the same line of business, we could work up some division of labor whereby one of them could think up the ideas, another could arrange them in

You can't get a world market without personal contact. This is why I feel that my five-year plan may take six. I shall have to do so much traveling.

notes, another could lose the notes, and yet another could hunt for them. This would take a lot of work off my hands and yet save time for the combination.

By then we would be ready for a fifth member of the pool to walk up and down the room dictating the story from such of the notes as can be found, while a sixth took it down in shorthand. We could all then get together and try to figure out the shorthand, with a special typing member ready to put the story down on paper in its final form. All that would now remain would be to put the stories in envelopes and address them, and it is here that I would fit in. That neat printing that I have been doing on blank checks all my life could be turned to good account here. It makes a great difference with an editor whether or not the contribution is neat, and it might turn out that I was the most important member of the pool. I don't think there is any doubt that the stories would be better.

So much for production. With my financial system reorganized and my production speeded up, the problem would be my world market. Here is where the fun would come in. You can't get a world market without personal contact. You couldn't very well write letters to people in Germany and Spain and say: "I am a little boy forty years old and how would you like to buy a piece that I have written?"

You would have to *go* to Germany and to Spain and see the people personally. This is why I feel that my five-year plan may take possibly six years to carry out. I shall have to do so much traveling to establish a world market. And I *won't* want any of my associates in the pool along with me, either. They will have plenty to do with thinking up ideas at home—and writing them.

Now, I may have this five-year plan all wrong. I haven't read much about Russia's, except to look at pictures showing Lenin's tomb. But I do know that the principle of the thing is that five years are supposed to elapse before anyone can really judge of its success. In five years Russia expects to have increased its production of wheat to 3,000,000,000,000 bushels (or is it 3,000,000,000?) and before that time everyone has got to take Russia's word for it. This is what appeals to me about the idea. I want to be given a little rest from all this nagging and eyebrow-lifting and "What about that article you promised?" and "Your account shows a slight overdraft." I want to have something definite to hold out to these people, like: "In five years' time I will have my whole system reorganized, with a yearly production of 3,000,000 articles and monthly deposits of $500,000. Can't you have a little faith? Can't you see that a great economic experiment is being carried on here?" (This, I think, ought to do the trick, unless they have no interest in progressive movements at all. And, from what I hear about them, they haven't.)

*Y*arns of

an *I*nsurance *M*an

I WAS talking with an old friend of mine, an insurance man, the other day (oh, well, maybe it wasn't quite the other day—just before America entered the war, it was) and trying to convince him that it would be bad business for his company to write me one of those twenty-payment-life policies (with time-and-a-half for overtime), when he suddenly turned to me and said: "Old man, did I ever tell you some of the strange accidents that insurance men run up against?"

I told him that he *had*, and tried to change the subject. But he was in a mood to be entertaining, whether he entertained or not, so I drew his chair up to the fire (hoping he would fall in) and he began: "You would hardly believe some of the unusual accidents which an insurance company is called upon to settle for," he said, jogging me slightly to awaken me, for I had traveled all day on horseback and was dog-tired.

"Whazzat?" I asked, starting up.

"I say you would hardly believe some of the unusual accidents that an insurance company is called upon to settle for," he repeated. "But, whether you will hardly believe them or not, I have a good mind to tell you. It will do you no harm to know how the other half lives."

"Did it ever occur to you that I *am* the other half?" I countered, falling asleep.

He ignored my sally. (By the way, I wonder what's become

of Sally.) "I remember once being called out in the dead of night to go and investigate a case where a client claimed to have thrown his collar bone out by trying to pull a Pullman blanket up around his shoulders during a cold night on the ride from Bagdad, California, to Los Angeles. He was—"

"But I thought that it was never cold in California," I said in my inimitable way.

"That is why we were suspicious. Our California man said that this would be impossible unless the man had caught a cold somewhere in the East and brought it with him to California. 'An ordinary chill, incident to an attack of grippe contracted in the East' was the way his report read. But the fact remained that the man *had* thrown his shoulder out and was in a hospital.

"So I hopped aboard a west-bound covered wagon, and, after various exciting adventures with the Indians in the Santa Fe station at Albuquerque (from which I emerged with a dozen bows and arrows and three Indian blankets at the unbelievable price of $150), I arrived at the hospital where our man was presenting his claim."

"And did the queen's archers win the tournament, daddy?" I asked, awakening from my doze.

"There was yet another case," he continued, "which involved the claim of a man who was run over by a glacier. He was a botanist, traveling in Switzerland, and had found a very rare species of edelweiss growing in a cranny near the Mer de Glace. It was impossible to pull it up by the roots, so he lay down on his stomach, with his back to the glacier, to examine its structure. As he lay there he got to daydreaming of what would have happened if he had married that girl and stayed in Utica when he was young, and from there got to reminiscing about the different sorts of candy he used to buy when a kid, the licorice sticks, hore-hound, wine cups, and all the rest, and, although his ribs got a little lame from lying on them, he got so wrapped up in his reveries that he didn't notice the glacier creeping up on him. He felt something crowding him slightly, but thought nothing of it at the time, attributing it to nervousness on his part. It was in this way that the river of ice finally ran over him and jammed one hip quite badly, to say nothing of giving him chilblains and quite a fright."

"I should think that an affair like that would come under the head of occupational disease," I said, nodding my head sagely. "Wouldn't his employers be responsible?"

"He had no employers. He was a botanist in for himself," said my friend. (I call him my friend, although I would gladly have been rid of him.)

"I understood you to say that he was a man trying to pull his blanket up around his shoulders on a Pullman," I said, in some (but not much) surprise.

"That, my friend, is another story which I will tell you sometime. Right now I want to cap the climax of my last yarn with the rather comical one about a certain Elwood M. Rovish, age 42, who asked reimbursement for damages suffered from ostrich-bane."

"Ostrich-bane?" I could hardly keep myself from asking—but I did.

"Mr. Rovish had been attending a class dinner and had started home about four A.M. on a steam roller which happened to be standing for the night in a near-by roadway. At nine o'clock the next morning he was awakened by a ring at his doorbell, and, on opening the door, he was confronted by a man who said:

"'Here is your ostrich.'

"Mr. Rovish said, as nicely as he could for the aspirin which was in his mouth, that he thought there must be some mistake, as he owned no ostrich, being a bachelor and living alone in a two-room apartment.

"'Oh yes you do own an ostrich,' replied the man. 'You bought him last night.'

"Well, to turn an anecdote into a long story, it transpired that Mr. Rovish on his way home had alighted from his steam roller at an ostrich farm, climbed over the fence, and mounted one of the fancier animals for a brisk ride about the place. The bird had put up quite a fight, with the result that the bird had been quite badly damaged as to plumage and pride. The owner had rushed out and insisted that, since Mr. Rovish seemed so fond of the ostrich, it would be well if he paid for it, and a sale was effected then and there, with the man agreeing to deliver the animal at Mr. Rovish's the next day. And here he was."

"I am fascinated," I said.

"As the man would, under no conditions, take the damaged bird back, Mr. Rovish was obliged to take it up into his two-room apartment, where, in the course of a week or so, it ate most of his shirts out of his bureau drawer and in general distressed his new owner and made it impossible for him to sleep. He then applied to his local agent for reimbursement on the grounds of 'ostrich-bane,' against which, unfortunately for us, he had been foresighted enough to insure himself. But I thought that it was a rather amusing story, and that you would be glad to hear it."

"*You* thought," I said. "Well, it wasn't. But before you go (and you *are* going, aren't you, old chap?) there is one thing I would like to insure myself against."

"And what is that?" said the agent, all smiles and policy forms.

"Against insurance agents!" I fairly screamed. "And against just such losses of time as I have just suffered."

And I'll be darned if he didn't write me out the policy.

More Work Ahead

AND now, with all this work that I have on my hands, along comes the Hoover Dam. I said to them when they came to me: "You'll have to get somebody else to build it. I've got work enough ahead now to keep me busy until September." But no. They must have me. So here I am—stuck with the job. And the funny part of it is, I never built a dam in my life.

I think what I will do is this: I will draw up all the plans and get things into running order and then I will turn the whole thing over to one of my lieutenants and say: "Lieutenant, here is one of the biggest jobs a man could ask for—bigger, in fact. I have laid everything out for you—here are the blue prints, here are the maps of the Colorado (the dam *is* to be on the Colorado, isn't it?), and you will find the sugar and coffee on the top shelf in the kitchen closet. Now go to it, boy, and make a name for yourself!" Then I will go back to bed.

Now we come to laying out the plans. The building of the Hoover Dam is no dilettante job. We have all got to keep sober—except, of course, Saturdays and Sundays. We can't have any kidding around the shop or any practical jokes, like joshing up the blue prints with "X marks the spot" and "Eddie loves Mabel." Those blue prints have got to tell a story, and they have got to tell it right. Otherwise the valley of the Colorado River will wake up some morning and find itself full of bluefish and old rowboats. Each and every one of us on the job has got to work like the very devil and just make this the best dam that has ever been built. I don't have to tell you boys that.

The first thing to do, as I see it, is to find the river. I know in a general way where it is, having stopped off for a day on the way to Hollywood to look at the Grand Canyon. (Don't tell me at this late date that *that* Colorado River isn't the one we're working on. That *would* discourage me.) As I remember it, it looked pretty big. Almost too big. Thinking back on what I saw that day, I have almost a mind to give the whole thing up. . . . Oh, well, the hell with it! Let's take a chance, anyway.

Now, once we decide on which river it is we are going to dam, the next thing to do is to decide how we are going to dam it. According to the specifications which have been turned over to me by the government the dam must be 730 feet high (I think that we can get away with 700 feet, which is a round number and easier to remember) and 1,100 feet long. That is pretty long. It is the longest dam *you* ever saw and I wouldn't be surprised if it was the longest dam that Hoover ever saw, engineer that he is. The canal (this is the first I have heard about a canal, by the way. I thought we were just building a dam)—the canal has got to be 200 miles long and big enough to float a ship drawing twenty feet of water. I am sorry to have to intrude all these technical details, but, after all, we are embarked on a fairly technical venture. You can't go at this thing as you would at making a punch or a costume for a fancy dress ball. We have got to *know* something about what we are going to do. Otherwise people will laugh.

You see, we plan to spend about $100,000,000 on the thing. This is the figure which the government has given me, but I plan on slipping a little bit more over because of the fact that we shall all have to have our lunches out there on the job and will naturally be expected to use taxis to get to and from work. I should think that a concern as big as the United States government would want its employees to be well nourished and travel in some sort of style, if only for appearances' sake. So we'll call it $100,000,750. If they don't

We are embarked on a technical venture. You can't go at this thing as you would at making a punch.

like it, they can protest it and we'll settle for the taxi fare. I, for one, do not intend to live right by the construction work. There must be a good hotel somewhere up back in the hills. If there isn't, we'll build one.

Now. Here we are, all set to begin. We have $100,000,000 to spend (with extras), a pretty fair-sized river to dam, and a lot of mending to be done. O.K. Let's go!

I frankly haven't the slightest idea of what to do first. (Don't let this get around!) My first idea would be to throw a lot of stuff into the river at the point where the dam is to be until it all fills up and we can go home. This is not as easy as it sounds. To begin with, we have got to get stuff to throw in which will not melt or filter through. This eliminates mud and corn husks. Mud is all right for a small dam, such as the ones we have built before, but this time we have got to allow for erosion, adhesion, collusion, and depreciation. All of which have to be divided by seven and taken the square root of. So we can't use mud; or, if we do, we have got to be careful and not call it mud in the expense account. When you are spending $100,000,000 you can't have an item like "Mud . . . $5,000,000." Congress would get suspicious.

All right, then. . . . The only thing left for us to do, that I can see, is to throw in a lot of concrete. And here is where our first big problem presents itself. How do we get the concrete into such form that we can throw it into the river so that it will stay? This, I admit, is a poser. We have simply got to mix the concrete up on the bank and throw it in great blocks where we want it. But how are we to get the blocks in the *middle* of the stream? The ends are all right. We can do that in no time. But that middle? I don't like to be a defeatist, but I doubt very much if it can be done at all.

If we go on this theory, *viz.*, that it can't be done at all, we are adopting the Lazy Man's attitude. What would have happened if Fulton had said: "I can't invent the steam engine?" What would have happened if Edison had said: "I can't beat Ford and Firestone at throwing horseshoes?" The work of this world has been done by men who said: "I can't"—and who *meant* it.

So now that we have got that old Colorado River just chock full of concrete blocks right where it needs it most, we must look around for some place to sit down and rest. And, unless I am very much mistaken, this is going to be our toughest job. You can't stand on the bank, as we shall have been doing, mixing concrete blocks and tossing them into a river, without making a frightful mess on the shores, what with donkey engines, concrete mixers, lemon peels, and White Rock bottles. What we shall have to do is to put in a requisition, or petty-cash voucher, for a man to pick all these things up and cart them away, so that we can sit down and rest when we have finally got the dam built.

We don't want to go back to the hotel right away, because something might happen. The dam might burst and you know what that means. Ask the people of Johnstown. They are still sore about it.

The government said nothing about it in the prospectus it sent to me, but I understand from friends that the district in which the dam is to be built gets pretty hot in summer. I have heard 120 in the shade quoted. They always add: "but, of course, it is that clear, dry heat—so you don't mind it." But I have heard that before. Natives are always telling you that the heat in their home town is clear and dry and that one doesn't notice it, but I have never been able to catch it on one of its clear, dry days.

My theory is that when it is 120 in the shade it is 120 in the shade, and I have pretty good scientific backing for my point. And 120 in the shade is too hot for work, wet or dry.

So, as far as I am concerned, things look pretty black for ever getting the Hoover Dam finished. We have, in this little summary, found that it is too big, too difficult, and too hot. That leaves practically nothing in its favor except that it might possibly be fun to tinker around with, which, you will admit, is nothing to sink $100,000,000 in.

My advice to the government (in sending in my resignation herewith) would be to drop the whole business before it is too late and stick to seeds.

*I*ll *W*ill *T*oward *M*en

NOBODY would like to see the Brotherhood of Man come to pass any more than I would, for I am not a very good fighter and even have difficulty holding my own in a battle of repartee. I am more the passive type, and I would be glad to have everybody else passive too.

But I am afraid that it can't be done. I am afraid that there are certain situations in which a man finds himself placed by chance where there is nothing left for him to do but hate his fellow man. It isn't that he wants to hate him, but certain chemical reactions take place in his system.

Take, for example, the case of a dining car. You come in alone and the steward waves the menu at you in a friendly fashion indicating that you are to sit right down here opposite this gentleman. At the very start, this gentleman resents your sitting opposite him and you resent his having got there first.

He doesn't take a good look at your face, or you at his, but you both concentrate an ugly glare on the buttons of each other's waistcoats. If he happens to have a fraternal watch charm on his chain you appraise it critically and say to yourself, "Oh, one of *those*, eh?" In the meantime, he has worked his inspection up to your tie, and you are conscious of the fact that he doesn't like it at all.

You take a quick look at what he is eating. It is usually steak and French-fried potatoes, with sliced tomatoes on the side. Has the guy no imagination in eating? You feel sure that he is going to top off with a piece of apple pie and a large cup of coffee. In the meantime, it has come your time to order. Now it is *his* turn to be critical.

As a matter of fact, that steak of his looks pretty good, but you wouldn't order that for a million dollars. He would know that you got the idea from him and you won't give him that satisfaction. So you order the deviled beef bones— and realize that he is laughing nastily to himself at your naïveté. The hell with him!

While your order is being prepared, you try looking out the window, but it is too dark to see anything. Here is the chance to break down the ill feeling slightly and make some remark, such as, "Dark out, isn't it?" But, unless you do it right away, the chance is lost and it is war to the death.

When your dinner comes, the advantage is all his. He can watch you serve yourself, make mental notes on *your* handling of your knife and fork, laugh inwardly at your attempts to get meat from a bone which has no meat on it. The result is that you spill large pieces of beef on the cloth, suddenly become self-conscious about holding your implements until you aren't sure just how you *have* been holding them all your life and, with the nervousness of a beginner, let your knife fly out of your hand on to the window sill. You are tempted to throw it at him, but you notice that he has divined your purpose and is grasping his. Well, let us have no bloodshed here. You can get him out in the vestibule.

Here are two citizens of the United States who should be brothers in the bond, whipped up to a state of mutual dislike and animosity without a word being spoken. He delays over his dessert much longer than he has to, and although you yourself would like some preserved figs with cream, you decide that one hog at a table is enough. You both pay your checks at the same time and sneer at each other's tip. Fortunately his car is in one direction from the diner and yours is in the other, so actual physical combat is avoided.

*He unfolds his paper and opens it so wide that it knocks your
hat askew.*

In elevators also we find a spirit which, without any justification whatsoever, threatens to destroy all the good work
which evangelists and philanthropists have been struggling
at all these years. Two people alone in an elevator, and
strangers to each other, are instinctive enemies. If one says:
"Ten out" and the other can beat him by two and say
"Eight out," it is a victory which can hardly be measured
by ordinary standards. Sidelong glances of hatred are shot
across the car. If one catches the other looking in the mirror,
a scornful leer passes over his face and the word "Siss" is
spoken just as clearly as if the sound were actually made.
If a woman gets into the car, and No. 1 takes off his hat
while No. 2 keeps his on, the first man boils with a desire
to snatch the other's hat from his head and dash it to the
floor, while the second does everything but sneer out loud
at the affectation which prompts the other to assume a
gentility which is both spurious and unnecessary.

The only thing which can possibly bring these two together
is the entrance into the car of two other people who carry

on their conversation over the heads of the other passengers. Our two original antagonists could almost become friends under the irritation of having to listen to the new occupants' badinage.

But probably the most common of all antagonisms arises from one man's taking a seat beside you on a train, a seat to which he is completely entitled. You get in at Bog Shore and find a seat by yourself. At any rate, you get the window, and although you know that by the time the train reaches Flithurst the car will be taxed to its capacity, you put your hat down in the seat beside you.

At Flithurst a long line of commuters files past. One of them, an especially unpleasant-looking man, spies your hat and hesitates. You are thinking: "The great hulk! Why doesn't he go on into the next car?" He is thinking: "I guess I'll teach this seat hog a lesson. . . . Is this seat taken?" Without deigning a reply, you grab your hat sulkily and cram it on your head. He sits down and the contest begins.

He unfolds his paper and opens it so wide that it knocks your hat askew. He is regarding the Post-Examiner. He *would*. Obviously an illiterate, to add to everything else. You crouch against the window sill, in exaggerated courtesy and fold your paper up into the smallest possible compass. Go ahead, take all the room if you want it! Don't mind *me*—oh, no! He doesn't. Nevertheless, he is boiling with antagonism, while you are on the point of pulling the bell rope and getting off the train to walk the rest of the way to town. And for what?

You are enraged because a man took a seat to which he was quite entitled, and he is enraged because he knows that you are enraged and, besides, you have the seat by the window. Thus we see that Old Stepmother Nature has her own ways and means of perpetuating warfare and hatreds. Every one of us may have a daily calendar with a motto on it about loving our fellow men, but when Nature puts two people within a radius of three feet of each other and turns on the current, there is no sense in trying to be nice about the thing. It is dog eat dog.

A *T*rip

to *S*pirit *L*and

In all the recent talk about spirits and spiritism (by "recent" I mean the past three hundred and fifty years) I have maintained what amounts to a complete silence, chiefly because I have been eating crackers a great deal of the time and couldn't talk, but also because I saw no reason for my giving away those secrets of spirit communication which have, in my day, made me known from Maine to New Hampshire as "the Goat of Ghosts." Now, however, I feel that society should know how it has been duped, hoop—doopa—duped, in fact.

I first began my experiments with spiritism in 1909 while sitting in the dark with a young lady who later turned out to be not my wife. Watches with phosphorescent dials had just come into use and I had one of the few in town. In fact, I had one of the few watches in town, most of the residents still sticking to the old-fashioned hourglass as being more handy. I had just moved my watch up to my nose to take a look at it in the dark, as I realized that it was time to go beddie-bye, when the young lady, seeing a phosphorescent blob of light make its way like a comet through the dark at her side, screamed, "There's a ghost in the room!" and fainted heavily.

It was some time before I could get out from under her, and even more time before I realized what it was that had given her such a fright; but, once it became clear to me, I knew that I had here the makings of a great little racket. So, stepping across her prostrate body, I went out into the world to become a medium, or, in the technical language of the craft, a medium stout.

Not many people realize how easy it is to fake spirit manifestations. For example, there was the famous case of one Dr. Rariborou, well known in London during the first decade of the century as a highly successful medium and eye-ear-nose-and-throat man. He combined his medical practice with his occult powers by making spirits play tambourines in people's throats while he was working on them. This not only mystified his patients but made them pretty irritable, so he had to give it up in the end and devoted all his time to séances.

Dr. Rariborou, or, as he afterward became known, "Dr." Rariborou, was famous for his "flying leg" trick, or "foot messages." This was a highly mystifying manifestation, even to Dr. Rariborou, although he knew exactly how it was done. The client was seated in a darkened room, after having examined the medium to make sure that he was securely bound with surgeon's tape to his assistant, who was, in turn, chained to the wall of the room. The room was then hermetically sealed, so that it got rather unbearable along about four o'clock.

Having made sure that everything was shipshape (one of those old medieval prison ships you read about—I don't), the client sat in a chair and held fast on to the knee of Dr. Rariborou. Sometimes they would sit this way for hours, if Dr. Rariborou happened to like the client. Otherwise, the séance would begin immediately with a message to the doctor from his control, an old Indian named Mike. Mike would tell the doctor that someone wanted to talk to the client, usually someone of whom the client had never heard, whereupon a ghostly leg would be seen flying through the air, delivering a smart kick with its foot on the side of the client's head. Almost simultaneously a kick would be received on the other side of the head, which would pretty well rock the client groggy. His chair would then be pulled out from under him and a pail of water be upset over his shoulders.

At the same time a spirit mandolin, suspended in mid-air, would play Ethelbert Nevin's Narcissus in double time, with not too expert fingering on the high notes.

This astounded, and bruised, a number of clients, and the doctor's reputation grew apace. The funny part of it was that practically every client who was thus maltreated had no difficulty in recalling some deceased friend or relative who might be glad to treat him in this manner. They all took it for granted that they were getting only what was coming to them from someone who was dead. They would say, as they picked themselves up after the séance: "I guess that must have been Dolly," or, "Sure, I know who *that* was, all right. It was Joe." All of which does not speak very well for human society as it is constituted today.

Now for the explanation of how this "flying leg" trick was done. It was one of my favourites when I was at the zenith of my powers. The medium is strapped, as we saw, by surgeon's tape, to his assistant, who is in turn chained to the wall. When the lights are put out, the medium, using the one knee which is free from the grasp of the client, presses a concealed spring in the chair on which he is sitting, which releases the entire side of the room to which the assistant is chained.

The assistant, with nothing to bother him now but the loose wall hanging to his wrists and the medium who is strapped to him, seizes an artificial leg which has been covered with phosphorescent paint and belabors the client with it as we have seen. With one foot he releases a spring which pulls the chair out from under the victim, and with the other foot releases another spring which upsets the pail of water. By this time the client doesn't know or care much what goes on.

Meanwhile the medium, still strapped to the assistant, brings out a mandolin pick which he has had concealed in his cheek and plays a phosphorescent mandolin which has been lowered by a second assistant from the ceiling to a point directly in front of his mouth. Narcissus calls for very little fretwork on the mandolin, being played mostly on the open strings, but what little fingering there is to be done is easily handled by the tip of the medium's nose which he has trained especially for this work. You can do it yourself some time, unless you happen not to like Narcissus as a tune. I myself got pretty darned sick of it after five or six years, which was one of the reasons I gave up holding séances.

Another famous medium, whose fakes are now generally recognized, was Mme. Wayhoo, an East Indian woman from New Bedford, Massachusetts, whose father was one of the old New Bedford whales. Her specialty was spirit writing, and her chief claim to integrity was that she herself could neither read nor write. (As a matter of fact, she was a graduate of Radcliffe, according to the gossips.) The person

His chair would then be pulled out from under him and a pail of water be upset over his shoulders.

desirous of getting in touch with deceased relatives would go into a darkened room and ask questions of Mme. Wayhoo, such as, "Is it in this room? Is it animal, vegetable, or mineral? Did you file an income-tax return in 1930 and, if so, were you married or single at that time?"

To these questions the medium would reply nothing, until the questioner got rather jittery as a result of sitting in a dark room and asking questions into the blackness with no replies. Just as some form of mental breakdown was about to take place, the medium would scratch on a slate with a slate pencil, at the revolting sound of which the client would leap into the air and rush from the room screaming. On returning, he or she would find that a message had been written on the slate, something like "Out to lunch—back at 2:30," or a complete bowling score. I do not even have to explain how this was done.

I have in my files hundreds of other explanations of psychic phenomena, but I am saving them up for a debate. I also have some excellent rye whisky which I will let go for practically nothing to the right parties.

*A*nnouncing

a *N*ew *V*itamin

Dr. Arthur W. Meexus and the author of this paper take great pleasure in announcing the discovery of vitamin F on August 15, 1931. We ran across it quite by accident while poking through some old mackerel bones, trying to find a little piece of fish that we could eat.

"By George," exclaimed Dr. Meexus, "I think this is a vitamin!"

"By George," I said, examining it, "it is not only a vitamin, but it is vitamin F! See how F it looks!" And, sure enough, it was vitamin F all over, the very vitamin F which had been eluding Science since that day in 1913 when Science decided that there were such things as vitamins. (Before 1913 people had just been eating food and dying like flies.)

In honor of being the first vitamin to be discovered, this new element was called vitamin A, and a very pretty name it was, too. From then on, doctors began discovering other vitamins—B, C, D, and E, and then vitamin G. But vitamin F was missing. It is true vitamin G looked so much like vitamin B that you could hardly tell them apart, except in a strong light, and vitamin E was, for all practical purposes, the same as vitamin A (except a little more blond), but nobody seemed able to work up any discovery by which a vitamin F could be announced.

The sad suicide of Dr. Eno M. Kerk in 1930 was laid to

the fact that he had just got a vitamin isolated from the
E class and almost into the F, when the room suddenly got
warm and it turned into a full-fledged vitamin G. The
doctor was heartbroken and deliberately died of malnutri-
tion by refusing to eat any of the other vitamins from that
day on. If he couldn't have vitamin F, he wouldn't have
any. The result was a fatal combination of rickets, beriberi,
scurvy, East Indian flagroot, and all other diseases which
come from an undersupply of vitamins (most of them diseases
which nice people up North wouldn't have).

First in our search for a vitamin which would answer to
the name of F, we had to figure out something that it would
be good for. You can't just have a vitamin lying around
doing nothing. We therefore decided that vitamin F would
stimulate the salivary glands and the tear ducts. If, for
instance, you happen to be a stamp licker or envelope sealer,
or like to cry a lot, it will be necessary for you to eat a great
deal of food which is rich in vitamin F. Otherwise your
envelopes won't stay stuck, or, when you want to cry, all
you can do is make a funny-looking face without getting
anywhere.

For research work we decided that the natives of one of
the Guianas (British-French, or French-British, or Harvard-
Yale) would present a good field, so we took a little trip
down there to see just what food values they were short of.
Most of the food in the Guianas consists of Guiana hen in
its multiple variants, with a little wild Irish rice on the side
to take away the taste. The natives reverse the usual order
of tribal eating, placing the hen and rice outside a large bowl
and getting into the bowl themselves, from which vantage
point they are able to pick up not only the food but any
little bits of grass and pebbles which may be lying on the
ground beside it. This method of eating is known as *hariboru*,
or "damned inconvenient."

Naturally, a diet consisting entirely of Guiana hen and
wild Irish rice is terribly, terribly short on vitamin F, with
the result that the natives are scarcely able to lick their lips,
much less a long envelope. And when they want to cry (as

they do whenever anyone speaks crossly to them) they make a low, grinding noise with their teeth and hide their eyes with one hand to cover up their lack of tears. We played them Silver Threads Among the Gold one night on our ukuleles, with Dr. Meexus singing the tenor, and although every eye in the house was dry, the grinding sound was as loud as the creaking timbers on an excursion boat. (As loud, but nothing like.)

The next thing to do was to discover what foods contain vitamin F. Here was a stickler! We had discovered it in a mess of mackerel bones, so evidently mackerel bones contain it. But you can't tell people to eat lots of mackerel bones.

Now, from a study of vitamins A, B, C, D, E, and G, we knew that all one really needs to have, in order to stock up on any one of these strength-giving elements, is milk. Milk and cod-liver oil. Milk has vitamin A, vitamins B, E, and G— so it is pretty certain to have vitamin F. For all we knew, it might also contain vitamin F sharp. So we picked milk as the base of our prescribed diet and set about to think up something else to go with it.

Then it occurred to Dr. Meexus that he had a lot of extra radishes growing in his garden, radishes which he was sure he had not planted. He had planted lots of other vegetables, beans, peas, Swiss chard, and corn, but radishes were the only things that had come up in any quantity. He was radish poor. And he figured out that practically six million amateur gardeners were in the same fix. Where you find one amateur gardener in a fix, you are pretty likely to find six million others in the same one. And, according to the Department of Agriculture's figures for 1931 (April-September), practically every amateur gardener in the country was in some sort of fix or other, mostly due to a bumper crop of radishes.

We therefore decided that radishes must contain a lot of Vitamin F, since they contain nothing else, unless possibly a corky substance which could be used only in the manufacture of life preservers. "Milk and radishes" was selected as the slogan for vitamin F.

We played them Silver Threads Among the Gold one night, with Dr. Meexus singing the tenor.

We figured it out that our chief advantage over the other vitamin teams was in the choice of conditions which our vitamin would cure. The vitamin B group had taken over beriberi, but who wants to have beriberi for a disease to be avoided? Vitamin D is a cure for rickets, but most of our patients ought to know by now whether they are going to have rickets or not. (We planned to cater to the more mature, sophisticated Long Island crowd, and, if they haven't had rickets up until now, they don't care much. If they *have* had them, it is too late anyway, and you can always say that your legs got that way from riding horseback.)

Vitamin C is corking for scurvy, but, here again, scurvy is not in our line.

In fact, I don't know much about scurvy, except that it was always found breaking out on shipboard when sailing vessels went around the Horn. But Dr. Hess, one of the discoverers of vitamin C, has pointed out that scurvy need not always be present in cases demanding vitamin C.

According to Hess (you must always call doctors who discover something by their last names without the "Dr."), the frequency among children in which irritability can be cured by vitamin C is proof that it has more uses than one.

This was pretty smart of Hess to pick on such a common ailment as irritability among children, for, up until the discovery of vitamin C, the only cure for this had been a good swift smack on the face.

However, it looks now as if we were stuck with a perfectly good vitamin and nothing for it to cure. Licking stamps and crying aren't quite important enough functions to put a vitamin on its feet. We have announced its discovery, and have given to the world sufficient data to show that it is an item of diet which undoubtedly serves a purpose. But what purpose? We are working on that now, and ought to have something very interesting to report in a short time. If we aren't able to, we shall have to call vitamin F in, and begin all over again.

Hiccoughing Makes Us Fat

So many simple little actions have been recently discovered to be fattening, there is hardly any move we can make, voluntary or involuntary, which does not put on weight for us. We have been told that laughing makes us fat, that sleeping after meals makes us fat, that drinking water makes us fat (or thin, according to which day of the week you read about it); and, although I haven't seen it specifically stated, I have no doubt that it has been discovered that yawning and sneezing are in the class with all the rest of the fatty tissue builders (who, by the way, seem to be just the busiest little builders since the days when the pyramids were being thrown together).

But, if you will notice, all of these fatty functions are rather pleasant ones.

Laughing, dozing, and yawning are certainly lots of fun.

Though there may be some opposition to sneezing as a pastime, I am pretty sure that, if you will be quite honest, you will admit that a good rousing sneeze, one that tears open your collar and throws your hair into your eyes, is really one of life's sensational pleasures. You may say, "Oh, darn it!" in between sneezes and try to act as if you weren't enjoying it, but, as an old hay-fever sufferer, I know the kick that can lie in a good sneezing spell, provided you have the time to give to it and aren't trying to thread a needle.

In the midst of all these little pleasures of life which are to be denied us if we want to keep thin, it seemed to me that hiccoughing ought to be proved fattening, thereby introducing something we *don't* like to do. I don't know of anyone who has a good word to say for hiccoughing. It is pretty easy to prove that almost anything makes people fat. All you have to do is drag out the old cells and gland secretions and talk about how they secrete fat in the blood and hide it away for the winter months. If you can get a dog or a cat in a cage and can make them do whatever the thing is you are studying, you ought to be able to prove your point in about fifteen minutes.

They put a dog and a cat in cages side by side the other day, and made them awfully cross at each other by telling the dog what the cat had been saying about him and the cat what the dog was telling his cronies about her, and, by testing the animals' blood before and after the hard feeling began, they discovered that they were both quite a bit thinner by supper time. It wasn't stated what their weight was *after* supper, or when the two had made up their little tiff, but it is safe to say that they both put on about three pounds each. I've tried those reducing gags myself and all that they do is make me hungry.

However, as not many people know what hiccoughing really is—except that it is a damned nuisance—it will be perfectly safe to go ahead on the cellular theory for a starter. You must know that our wonderful Human Machine (wonderful except for about three hundred flaws which can be named on the fingers of one hand) is made up of countless billions of little cells called "cells," and that it is the special duty of some of these little body cells to store up fat. And I will say this for them: they do their duty.

I have got a set myself which lean over backward in their devotion to their duty. They must have little mottoes up on the walls of their workshop reading: Do It Now! and A Shirker Never Wins.

I sometimes think that they get other cells in from an agency to help them when it looks as if they weren't going to get their quota of fat secreted by five o'clock, for they haven't fallen down once on the job as yet. I wish I could say as much for the cells whose duty it is to *destroy* fat. I suspect that my fat-destroying cells drink, or else they don't get enough sleep. Something is slowing them down, I know that.

Now, let us say for the purposes of argument (not a very hot argument, just kidding) that the process of hiccoughing is a muscular reaction caused by an excess secretion of the penal glands (I made that one up, but there ought to be a penal gland if there isn't). You have been sitting, let us say, at a concert, or have been trying to play the flute, and have become exhausted. This exhaustion sets loose a nervous toxin which, in turn, sets loose five homing pigeons which try to fly out of your mouth. This is what we know as hiccoughs, or "the hicks."

If it were not for these hiccoughs, the fatigue poison set loose by the exhaustion would act on the cells and destroy great quantities of fat, making it necessary for us to take in our clothing two or three inches. But the hiccoughs, or escaping pigeons, step in and relieve the toxic condition, thereby leaving the fat where it was—and you know where *that is.* In my experiments I had no cats or dogs to place in cages, but I used an aunt who was visiting us and who hadn't been doing much around the house to pay for her keep. I placed her in a cage, and in the cage next to her placed a parrot which she insists on carrying about visiting with her wherever she goes. After testing the blood of both the aunt and the parrot and giving them some candy to keep them quiet, I tried to induce hiccoughs in the aunt. This was not so easy, as she didn't want to hiccough.

Now, hiccoughing is all very easy to fall into when you don't want to, but there doesn't seem to be any way in which to induce it out of thin air. I showed the aunt pictures of people hiccoughing, thinking to bring it on by suggestion. But she wouldn't look. I tried giving imitation hiccoughs myself, but succeeded only in bringing on an acute attack of real ones which I didn't want. (Unfortunately, I had neglected to test my own blood beforehand, so these were of no use in the experiment.)

My own hiccoughing, however, got my aunt to laughing, and that, together with the candy, set up quite a decent little attack of hiccoughs. This, in turn, excited the parrot, who was accustomed to mock my aunt to the point of rudeness, and he began a series of imitation hiccoughs which were as irritating as they were unskillful.

Things went on like this for several days, when finally the parrot gave up the whole thing and took to singing instead. My aunt and I were spasmodically hiccoughing, but it was nothing to what it had been when the fit was at its height.

I am sure you will admit that a good rousing sneeze is one of life's sensational pleasures.

In fact, I had plenty of time between hiccoughs to make blood tests of the aunt and to try to make one of the parrot. The parrot, however, would have none of it, and so I am unable to report on the effect of hiccoughing on the weight of birds.

As far as my aunt goes (and that is pretty far) I have data to show that she gained four pounds during the seizure, owing entirely to the elimination of the fat-destroying poisons through the agency of hiccoughing.

Thus we find that all fattening pastimes are not pleasurable. This is going to revolutionize the science of weight reduction, for the whole thing has been hitherto based on the theory that we mustn't do the things we want to do and must do the things we dislike (I mention no names in this latter group, but certain forms of lettuce and green vegetables will know whom I am referring to). Now, if we are to keep from doing even one disagreeable thing, like hiccoughing, the whole tide may turn, and by 1933 it may be so that the experts will tell us *not* to do the unpleasant things (and then where will you be, my fine lettuce?) and to go in strong for everything that gives us pleasure.

A Little Sermon

on *Success*

A FAMOUS politician once remarked, on glancing through a copy of Jo's Boys by Louisa M. Alcott, that he would rather have written Three Men in a Boat than to have dug the Suez Canal. As a matter of fact, he never did either, and wasn't quite as famous a politician as I have tried to make out. But he knew what he meant by Success.

Lord Nelson is quoted as having said to one of his subordinates just before he went into action that there was no such thing as a good war or a good peace; in fact, that he doubted if there was a good anything. Now, Lord Nelson was a successful man in the sense that the world means Success, but he was unhappy because he had on his conscience the fact that he had imprisoned those two little princes in the Tower of London and had been instrumental in having them dressed in black velveteen and wear long blond curls like a couple of sissies. He was a successful man, but had only one eye.

I could go on indefinitely citing examples of great men who said things. I guess I will.

One hundred and seventy-five years ago General Wolfe Montcalm (sometimes called General Wolfe and sometimes General Montcalm, but always found on the Plains of Abraham) wrote to his adjutant: "I sometimes wonder what it is all about, this incessant hurry-scurry after Fame. And how are *you*, my dear adjutant? And that bad shoulder of yours? Look out for that. And look out for a girl named Elsie, who may drop in on you and say that she knows me. She doesn't know me at all; in fact, who of us can say that he really knows anyone else? I often wonder if I know myself."

There was a great deal more to the letter, but I have quoted enough to show that the famous general saw through the phantom which men call Success. He won Quebec, but, after all, what is Quebec? He had to pay eight to ten, and even then he had that long hill to climb. His knowledge of what Life really means came too late for him, just as it comes too late for most of us.

There is a tribe of head-hunters who live in the jungle of Africa who reverse the general practice of seeking Success. When they are little babies they are all made head of the tribe, the highest office known in the jungle, and are given great bags full of teeth (the medium of exchange corresponding to our money, only not so hard to get and certainly not

Lord Nelson was unhappy because he had imprisoned
those two little princes in the Tower.

so easy to get rid of, for who wants a lot of teeth around the house?).

The idea then is for each young man to spend his life trying to get out of the office of tribal head, to dispose of his legal tender, and to end up in the gutter. The ones who succeed in doing this are counted the happy ones of the tribe, and it is said that they are "successful" men. The most successful man in the history of the tribe ended up in the gutter at the age of seven. But he had luck with him. He lived in the gutter anyway and all that he had to do was to lie over.

Now, perhaps these head-hunters have the right idea. Who knows? Charles Darwin once said that it isn't so much the Little Things in Life which count as the Little Life in Things. The less life there is in a man, the happier he is, provided there aren't mosquitoes in the room and he can get his head comfortable. (If Charles Darwin didn't say that, it is the first thing he *didn't* say.)

People often come to me and ask what I would recommend for this and that, and I ask them, "This and that what?" And they go away sadly and think me a very wise man. I am not a wise man. I am just a simple man. "Simple Simon" they used to call me, until they found out that my name is Robert. I take Life as it comes, and although I grouse a great deal and sometimes lie on the floor and kick and scream and refuse to eat my supper, I find that taking Life as it comes is the only way to meet it. It isn't a very satisfactory way, but it is the *only* way. (I should be very glad to try any other way that anyone can suggest. I certainly am sick of this one.)

Once upon a time, in a very far-away land, before men grew up into the little boys they are now (Emerson once said that a little boy is just the lengthened shadow of one man), there was a very, very brave Knight who had a very, very definite yen for a beautiful Princess who lived in a far-away castle (very, very far away, I mean).

Now, there was also in this same land a Magician who could do wonders with a rabbit. People came from far and

The Magician began to pull paper roses out of the landlord's neck, much to the delight of everyone except the landlord.

near to watch him at his egg-breaking and card-dropping, and now and again someone from the country would cry out, "Pfui!" But for the most part he was held to be as good as that feller who came down from Boston once. And, by one of those strange oddments of Fate which so often bring people together from the ends of the earth, the Magician was also in love with the very, very lovely Princess who lived you-know-where.

And it happened that the Knight went riding forth one day on his milk-white charger (or, at any rate, he had been milk-white until he thought it would be comical to lie down and roll in his stall) and set out to find the Princess, whom he still thought the loveliest lady he had ever seen, although he had not yet seen her. He was a little in doubt as to which direction to take, for the Princess' castle, besides being very, very far away, was very, very hazy in the Knight's mind, he having heard of it only as "the Princess' castle" with no mention of its location. That's nothing to go by.

Now, at the same hour, the Magician himself was setting out on a horse he had brought out of a silk hat, bent on the same errand as the Knight—to get that Princess. And he, too, knew no more of where he was going than did the Knight—with the result that, after riding about in circles for three years, they both ended up at the same inn, eight miles from the town from which they started.

Now, the Knight was very fond of magic and the Magician was very fond of Knights. So, after a few tankards of mead together, the Magician got out his kit and began to pull paper roses out of the landlord's neck, much to the delight of everyone present except the landlord, who said that it was done with mirrors.

And so the Knight and the Magician became bosom friends and forgot about the very, very lovely Princess, and the Knight took the Magician home with him to his castle, so that every evening he could have another sleight-of-hand show. And the Princess, who by this time had got pretty sick of waiting, went back to her husband—who, it must be admitted, was a little disappointed at the way things had turned out.

Now, this little fable shows us that Success may be one of two things: first, getting what we want; and, second, *not* getting what we want.

It was Voltaire who is reported to have said: "*Plus ça change—plus ça reste*," meaning, "There isn't much sense in doing anything these days." Perhaps it wasn't Voltaire, and perhaps that isn't what the French means; but the angle is right.

Can you say the same of yourself?

*Y*esterday's
*S*weetmeats

It is a rather dangerous thing to note encouraging tendencies in our national life, for just as soon as someone comes out with a statement that we are better than we used to be, we suddenly prance into another war, or a million people rush out and buy Crude Oil, preferred, or there is an epidemic of mother murders, and we are right back in the neolithic age again with our hair in our eyes.

But in the matter of children's candy I am afraid that we shall have to come right out and say definitely that the trend is upward. When I look back on the days of my youth and remember the candy that I used to impose on my stomach, the wonder is that I ever grew up to be the fine figure of a man that I now am. The wonder is that I ever grew up at all. Perhaps that was the idea, and I fooled them.

There were two distinct brands of candy in my day: the candy you bought in the drug store on Sunday, when the candy shops were closed, and the week-day, or Colored Corrosion, brand, which, according to all present-day standards of pure food, should have set up a bright green fermentation, with electric lights, in the epiglottises of nine-tenths of the youth of that time.

We can dismiss the Sunday drug-store candy with a word, for it was bought only once a week and then only for lack of something better. Its flavor was not enhanced by the fact that it was kept in tall glass jars, like appendixes, down at the end of the store where the prescriptions were filled, and consequently always had a faint suspicion of spirits of niter and sod. bicarb. about it.

The delicacy called "calves foot," for instance, which came in long ridged sticks, to be sucked with little or no relish, not only tasted of old French coffee on the second or third brewing, but gave you the undesirable feeling that it was also good for sore throat. The Sunday licorice sticks were larger and more unwieldy, and were definitely bitter on the tongue, besides costing a nickel apiece. Although the rock candy was sweet, it lacked any vestige of imagination in its make-up and made the eating of candy a hollow mockery, and, of course, horehound was frankly medicinal and could be employed only when everything else had failed.

It was on week days that the real orgy of poisoned and delicious candy took place, a dissipation which was to make a nation of dyspeptics of the present generation of business men and political leaders. This candy was usually bought in a little store run by an old lady (probably an agent in the employ of the German government, in a farsighted scheme to unfit the American people for participation in the war which was to come), and your arrival was heralded by the jangle of a little bell not very cleverly concealed on the top of the door. This was followed by a long period of concentration, the prospective customer sliding his nose along the glass case from end to end, pausing only to ask the price of particularly attractive samples. The smell of those little candy shops is probably now a vanished scent of a bygone day, for it combined not only the aroma of old candies and leather baseballs, but somehow the jangle of the little bell entered into one's nostrils and titillated two senses at once.

In this collection of tasty morsels the one which haunts my memory most insistently is a confection called the "wine cup," a cone-shaped bit of colored sugar filled with some villainous fluid which, when bitten, ran down over the chin and on to the necktie. It was capped by a dingy piece of marshmallow which was supposed to be removed with the teeth before drinking the ambrosia within, but usually at the first nibble the whole structure collapsed, with the result that inveterate "wine-cup" consumers had a telltale coating of sugared water down the front of the coat, and, on a cold day, a slight glaze of ice on the chin. What went on in the stomach no one knows, but it does not make a very pretty picture for the imagination.

Another novelty was an imitation fried egg in a small frying pan, the whole sticky mess to be dug out with a little tin spoon which always bent double at the first application and had to be thrown away. The procedure from then on was to extract the so-called "egg" with the teeth, with the chin jammed firmly into the lower part of the "frying pan" as a fulcrum. This, too, left its mark on the habitué, the smear sometimes extending as high up as the forehead if the nose was very small, as it usually was.

There was one invention which was fortunately short-lived, for even in those days of killers' candy it was a little too horrible for extended consumption. It consisted of two cubes (the forerunner of our bouillon cubes of today) which, on being placed each in a glass of water and mixed with a soda-fountain technique, proceeded to effervesce with an ominous activity and form what was known either as "root beer," "ginger ale," or "strawberry soda," according to the color of the cubes.

The excitement of mixing them was hardly worth the distinct feeling of suicide which accompanied the drinking of the result, for God knows what they were or what the chemical formula for the precipitate could have been. Probably something which could have gone into the manufacture of a good, stable house paint or even guncotton.

The little mottoes, in the shape of tiny hearts, which carried such varied sentiments as "I Love You," "Skiddoo," "Kick Me," and "Kiss Me Quick," were probably harmless enough in their make-up, although I would always mistrust anything colored pink, but transporting them from shop to school and around the town loose in the pocket soon rendered them grimy and covered with gnirs (a "gnir" is a little particle of wool found in the bottom of pockets,

*The excitement of mixing them was hardly worth the distinct
feeling of suicide which accompanied drinking the result.*

especially constructed for adhering to candies) and unfit
for anything involving an æsthetic sense.

"Chocolate babies" also made poor pocket candies, especially when in contact with "jelly beans." (The "jelly bean"
seems to have survived down the ages and still is served in
little bean pots from the original stock in the store. It would
be interesting to discover why.) Licorice whips and "all-day
suckers" (which changed color and design on being held in
the mouth, a fact which seemed miraculous at the time, but
which, on contemplation, sends a slight shudder down the
middle-aged spine) were probably the safest of all early
twentieth-century candies, but even they would probably
fail miserably to pass the test of the Bureau of Standards at
Washington.

Worst of all was the "prize package," a cone of old newspaper containing the odds and ends of the day's refuse—hard
marshmallows with enough thumbprints on them to convict

the candy dealer ten times over, quantities of tired pop corn which had originally been pink, strange little oddments of green and red sugar which, even in their heyday, could not have been much, and, as the Prize, either a little piece of tin in the approximate shape of a horse or a button reading "Bust the Trusts." My gambling instinct made these "prize packages" a great favorite for my pennies, and it is to these and to old Mrs. Hill, who ran the candy shop and dispensed her largesse in this great-hearted manner, that I lay my present inability to eat eggs which have been boiled for more than eight seconds. Dear, *dear* Mrs. Hill!

And so, regardless of the present generation's freedom and reputed wildness, I will take a chance on their stomachs being in better shape at forty than mine is, for bootleg alcohol, whatever its drawbacks, takes away that craving for sweets which was the ruin of my generation.

$\mathcal{D}$efying
the $\mathcal{C}$onventions

WITH the advent of the political conventions there are three courses left open to the General Public (recently reduced to Major General Public on a private's pay). The private citizen who is not impressed by these two great gatherings of nominators may (1) tell the boy to stop leaving the morning and evening papers until further notice; (2) go up into the attic and hide in a trunk until it is all over; (3) go to the conventions in person, take a seat well up front, and when, if ever, there comes a moment of comparative quiet, deliver a long and resounding "bird," using one of those rubber contraptions especially designed for the purpose. Perhaps if enough private citizens went to the conventions in person there would be no room for the delegates and then we wouldn't have to have any election!

But since there is small chance of getting enough volunteers to crowd out the regulars, we might as well brush up on the details of how, according to the Constitution (the document, not the frigate), our Presidential candidates are nominated. We learned all about this in school, of course, but we also learned how to erect a square on the hypotenuse of a right-angled triangle and prove something by it—and where did *that* get us? I could entertain you for hours telling you where my geometry got me, but this is a political treatise.

According to the Constitution (the frigate, not the document), "each state will appoint, or shall cause to be appointed, or shall appoint to be caused, or shall go jump in the lake, as the legislature thereof may direct—" I guess that isn't the clause.

Anyway, every four years (it seems oftener, but that is because time passes so quickly when you are enjoying yourself), every four years a mysterious list of names appears in the papers, names of people who claim to be "delegates," seemingly empowered to go to the conventions, eat nuts, and

My personal theory is that they were changed from mice into delegates by a good fairy who got to changing pumpkins into coaches and couldn't stop.

vote for candidates for the Presidency. Just how they became "delegates" nobody seems to remember, but there must have been some ritual gone through with at *some* time, otherwise they would be just ordinary citizens like the rest of us. And when I say "ordinary," do I mean *ordinary!*

There is one explanation of the problem of where their delegates come from in the theory that they are chosen by taking the names that were left over in the hat after the drawings for the Irish Sweepstakes. Another school of political economists claim that they were the first ten to send in post cards making the greatest number of words out of "K-L-E-E-N-C-H-I-N Toothpaste—No More—No Less." My personal theory is that they were elected by being changed from mice into delegates by a good fairy who got to changing pumpkins into coaches and couldn't stop.

At any rate, along about February every four years they spring up and begin giving off hints as to which one of the candidates they favor, or, as the kidding phrase goes, "are pledged to." The pledge of a delegate to a national convention is embossed on tissue paper and, when rolled up, can be exploded by pulling little strings at either end. Inside will be found a motto reading: "If in January you were born, then blow a toot upon this horn. I love you." This makes it clear which candidate they are supporting. The rule is that each candidate must either keep his pledge or else give it to someone who will keep it for him until he gets back.

At the conventions, the main feature is the marching around the hall. No one can be a delegate who cannot march around a hall and sing, "Hail, hail, the gang's all here!" This is what is known as the dignity of Democracy. There has been some talk of dispensing with the delegates entirely and just getting the Boys' Fife and Drum Corps of each community to go to the conventions bearing signs reading, "We want a touchdown!" and "Kiss me again!" thereby giving the same effect as the delegates and yet maintaining a certain feeling of genuine youth. If the idea is just to be boys again, why not get *real* boys and not fifty-year-old men in Ferris waists? A good convention of sixteen-year-old boys, with their girls, would be a relief. Then we should know where we stood.

The party system in the United States is rather complicated right now, owing to there being no parties and very little United States. The Republican and Democratic parties, ancient rivals, do not exist any more as such, there being more fun watching Harvard and Yale. This has brought about a condition where Republican conventions are sometimes attended by Democrats by mistake, and Democratic conventions attended by Republicans on purpose. The only way to tell them apart is by the conditions of the hotel rooms after the convention is over. The Republicans leave more gin bottles and the Democrats seem to have gone in more for rye.

The hotel room as a factor in the political conventions can hardly be overemphasized. The main assembly hall or auditorium (so called because no one can hear anyone talking in it) is used chiefly for the marching and fistfighting, with an occasional round dance or hockey game. It is here also that all the photographs are taken. In the 1936 conventions it is planned to use the photographs of the 1928 and 1932 conventions and not use the auditorium at all, just sticking to the hotel rooms where the real work of the session is done. In fact, in 1936 it may not be necessary for the delegates to go to the convention city at all. They can just stay at home and march up and down in their own rooms until instructions come from the leaders as to how they are to vote.

But, you may say, what about the applause? How can there be a convention without the regulation applause which lasts ten, fifteen, or twenty minutes as each candidate's name is mentioned? This is a tough one, but there ought to be some way around it. Each delegate, if he stayed in his own home town, could send a telegram reading, "I am applauding for fifteen minutes," or "Consider that I am giving the name of George W. Glib an ovation."

This, however, will probably never receive the support of the newspapers, as attending political conventions is the only form of fun that many reporters get. In fact, if it weren't for the newspapers there would be no convention at all. With a man from each paper or news syndicate to cover the political angle, the personality angle, the woman's angle, the ginger-pop angle, the angle angle (that word is beginning to look as if it weren't spelled right), the resultant unemployment among newspaper men if the convention were abolished would be frightful and might end up in a revolution. It has been estimated that at this year's conventions there will be more newspaper men than delegates, many of them depending on the hand-outs from the various headquarters for their sandwiches and coffee for the coming year.

A revolution of half-starved and wholly parched convention reporters would be the biggest thing since the Union Square riots.

Thus we find that, for the present at any rate, it will be necessary for the so-called "delegates" to take their instructions right in the convention city itself.

And when the whole thing is over and the radio programs have settled back into the regular run of pancake recipes and Oh, Sweet Mystery of Life, At Last I've Found You without being broken up by Alabama's twenty-four votes being announced every five minutes, and when all the bottles and sevens of spades have been picked up off the floor along with some of the older delegates who haven't been able to stand the heat, and when two candidates have been chosen to carry the banners of their respective parties in the great 1932 Presidential campaign—then we can start reading the papers again.

*W*hat of *E*urope?

HAVING just been brought back from a brief but painful survey of business conditions in Europe (by "Europe" I mean three or four hundred square feet in Paris and another good place in Rome), I am continually being besieged by bankers and manufacturers to tell them how things are faring with our cousins (I always insist that they are *not* our cousins except distantly through marriage) overseas. "Watchman, tell us of the night!" is the way the bankers and manufacturers phrase it as they accost me. "What of Europe? Will she survive?"

Rather than go on with these individual conferences in dingy financial establishments, I am putting all my answers down here, where he who reads may run, and the devil may take the hindmost.

To begin with, my economic survey of Europe notes a startling increase in blondes in Paris. Big blondes. Being a Nordic myself, I am accustomed to blondes; but the blondes with which the Paris market is now being glutted through Scandinavian and German dumping are larger than any that I remember ever having seen before, even among my own people. They run anywhere from five feet eleven to six feet three, with eyes and beam to match.

This sort of thing can't go on, you know, and still have civilization keep to its present standards. For not only are these Parisian blondes tall and powerful, but they are snooty

—very, *very* snooty—and it is as much as a medium-sized man's life is worth just to carry on a polite conversation with one of them. They seem to have no idea at all of bringing about friendlier relations between Europe and America—an indifference which is, to say the least, unfortunate at this time when Europe needs America so sorely.

Just why these amazons bother to come out of doors at all is a puzzle, for they don't seem to be enjoying a minute of it. They might much better be back in the army, knocking down privates and drilling people. On meeting one of them, with one of those little black hats hanging on the side of that blonde coiffure, one's first instinct is to stand at attention and salute. One's second instinct is to run. The second instinct is the better.

Now, with this sudden influx of blondes into a market which has hitherto specialized in brunettes, what may we expect the effect to be on the American market? (This is the question that is being asked *me*, mind you, by American business men. I, personally, don't care. I have my books and a good pipe, and I am looking around for a dog.) And, in order to answer this question, a little extra research is necessary. This is not so easy to accomplish.

If, by the use of ether or a good swift crack on the jaw, one can get close enough to these Parisian blondes to note the texture of the goods, one discovers that they are really *American* in manufacture. In other words, a large percentage of Parisian blondes are platinum, copied after the Jean Harlow model so popular in America last year. The *hauteur* is also an American model, distinctly Ziegfeld (before bad business made the Ziegfeld girls loosen up and smile a little out of one corner of their mouths), and the only real contribution that Europe has made to the present product is the size.

I cannot account for the size, for it certainly is not French, unless French girls have really been tall all the time and have just been walking along all crouched over until now. It must be that the Scandinavian countries and Germany are working night and day to turn out something that will sweep the

Not only are these Parisian blondes tall and powerful, but they are very, very snooty.

world markets, although, of course, Germany has no right to do this under the Versailles Treaty. Here is something that should be looked into by an interallied commission (if one can be got together which will not immediately start ripping off each other's neckties).

Another question which my clients on Wall Street and throughout the rest of the country are asking me is, "What about Italy under Mussolini?" This I cannot answer as comprehensively as I would like, because I do not speak Italian very well. (I can say "hello" and then "hello" again, in case they didn't understand me the first time, but aside from that my conversation is carried on by an intelligent twinkling of the eyes and nodding of the head to show that I understand what is being said to me. As I do *not* understand, I often get into trouble in this way.)

My chief criticism of Italy under Mussolini is that it is too Italian. It is all very well in America for tenors and other participants in a church festival who are supposed to be dressed in Neapolitan costumes to sing O Sole Mio and Santa Lucia, but you don't expect real Italians to do it. It is as if real Americans were to go about singing Yankee Doodle. O Sole Mio and Santa Lucia are the only Italian songs that members of a local American pageant know. They *have* to sing them. But surely there must be some others that Italians know, and you would think that they would want to sing them, if only to be different from the Americans. But no! They sing O Sole Mio and Santa Lucia, and seem to think they are doing something rather fine.

Furthermore, there is the question of spaghetti. In New York or San Francisco, when you go to an Italian restaurant, you expect to get spaghetti, because that is supposed to be the big Italian dish. Imagine the shock, on visiting Italy, to find that it *is* the big Italian dish! I am not averse to spaghetti, mind you, and in New York have been known to do rather marvelous things with it, both with and without my vest. But I am not a spaghetti fiend, and after a week in Italy I was ready to call it quits and taper off into wheat cakes and baked beans. But they won't let you.

They are all so proud of the way they (each individual spaghettist) fix the dish, that you must not only eat three platefuls at each meal, but you must smack your lips and raise your fork and say "Wonderful!" at each mouthful, for they are standing right over you and watching with tears in their eyes to see how you are taking it. My enjoyment of the thing was hampered by the fact that I always seemed to get a plate with a self-feeding arrangement in the bottom, whereby no matter how much I ate there was a steady flow up through the table which kept my plate constantly full. I could wind it around my fork or scoop it up in my spoon or shovel it into my mouth like ticker tape by the yard, but it made no impression on the mound before me.

I would estimate that in sheer yardage alone I consumed enough spaghetti to knit sixty or seventy white sweaters.

And always there was the *maestro* standing by beaming and asking, "Was good?" I finally had to resort to a little ruse whereby I would fall screaming to the floor as if in an epileptic fit and have myself carried out of the room away from that never-ending flow of pasta.

I don't think that I shall visit an Italian restaurant in New York again for ever and ever so long.

This excess of spaghetti and Italian love songs is made much worse by a Mussolini-bred efficiency which causes your various courses at a meal to be rushed in front of you before you have got the order, or the course you are eating, out of your mouth. Just as you begin coping with the noodles, you see the waiter rushing up with the macaroni, and behind him another waiter with the ravioli, and way down in the distance still a third with the cheese and fruit. It rather takes the heart out of one, especially a slow-moving American who likes to dawdle a bit over his food.

The money question in Europe is naturally the one in which American financiers are most interested. Leaving the silver standard out of it (a process which seems to be taking care of itself pretty well) and eliminating the gold supply as a factor, I would say that the question of money in European countries was just about the same as the question of money in America—a situation which can be summed up in two words: "Not enough."

What
Are Little Boys
Made Of?

DID you know that you have enough resin in your system to rub up a hundred violin A strings? Or enough linoleum to carpet two medium-sized rooms (without bath)? You were probably not aware of these valuable properties lying dormant in your physical make-up, and yet scientists tell us that they are there.

As you all were taught in school, our body is made up of millions and millions of tiny particles called the Solar System. These tiny particles are called "æons," and it would take one of them fifteen billion years to reach the sun if it ever broke loose and *wanted* to get to the sun.

Well, anyway, these millions and millions of tiny particles are composed of hydrogen, oxygen, iodine, phosphorus, Rhode Island, Connecticut. There is also a blueplate dinner for those who don't like iodine. The action of all these elements sets up a ferment (C_2HN_4, or common table pepper) which sometimes ends in digestion but more often does not. If any of these agents is lacking in our make-up, due to our having dressed in a hurry, we say we are "deficient," or perhaps we "feel awful." Even with everything working I don't feel so hot.

It is only recently that doctors have discovered that we have many more elements in our systems than was originally thought. Whether we have always had them and just didn't know it, or whether they were brought there and left by some people who wanted to get rid of them has not been decided.

They tell us that the average 150-pound body (and a very pretty way to phrase it, too) contains enough carbon alone to make 9,000 lead pencils (not one of them ever sharpened, probably).

Another item which the doctors tell us we have in abundance is hydrogen—"enough in excess," they put it, "to fill about a hundred child's balloons." There's a pretty picture for you! As if we didn't have troubles enough as it is, we must go about with the consciousness that we have the makings of one hundred child's balloons inside us, and that under the right conditions we might float right off our chairs and bounce against the ceiling until pulled down by friends!

Thinking of ourselves in terms of balloons, lead pencils, whitewash (we have enough lime in us to whitewash a chicken coop, says one expert), and matches (we are fools to bother with those little paper books of matches, for we are

Under the right conditions we might float off our chairs and bounce against the ceiling.

carrying around enough phosphorus to make 2,200 match heads), all this rather makes a mockery of dressing up in evening clothes or brushing our hair. We might just as well get a good big truck and pile ourselves into it in the raw whenever we want to go anywhere, with perhaps some good burlap bags to keep the rain off. There is no sense in trying to look nice when all that is needed is a sandwich-board sign reading: "Anything on this counter—15 cents."

And that is the ultimate insult that these inventory hounds have offered us: they tell us just how much all this truck of which we are made is worth in dollars and cents. They didn't have to do that. Put all our bones, brains, muscles, nerves, and everything that goes into the composition of our bodies on to scales and, at the current market prices, the whole lot would bring just a little over a dollar. This is on the hoof, mind you. If we wanted to tie each element up in little packages with Japanese paper and ribbon, or if we went to the trouble to weather them up a bit and call them antiques, we might be able to ask a little more.

For example, the average body, such as might meet another body comin' through the rye, contains only about one tenth of a drop of tincture of iodine at any one time, and one tenth of a drop would hardly be worth the dropper to pick it up for the retail trade. And yet, if *we* don't have that tenth of a drop something happens to our thyroid gland and we sit around the village grocery store all day saying "Nya-ya!" Or to our pituitary gland and we end up wearing a red coat in a circus, billed as Walter, the Cardiff Behemoth: Twice the Size of an Ordinary Man and Only Half as Bright.

I don't see why scientists couldn't have let us alone and not told us about this. There was a day when I could bounce out of bed with the lark (I sometimes let the lark get out first, just to shut the window and turn on the heat, but I wasn't far behind), plunge into a cold tub (with just a dash of warm to take off the chill), eat a hearty breakfast, and be off to work with a light heart.

But now I get out of bed very carefully, if at all, thinking of those 9,000 lead pencils which are inside me. Too much water seems to be a risk, with all that iron lying around loose. Exercise is out of the question when you consider 2,200 match heads which might jolt up against each other and start a very pretty blaze before you were halfway to work.

Suppose that we *are* as full of knickknacks as the doctors say. Why not let the whole matter drop and just forget about it? Now that they have put the thing into our heads, the only way to get it out is for some expert to issue a statement saying that everyone has been mistaken and that what we are really made of is a solid mechanism of unrustable cast iron and if anything goes wrong, just have a man come up from the garage and look it over.

*T*he *B*ig
*C*oal *P*roblem

A GREAT deal of thought has been devoted to the subject of how we are going to meet the problems of this winter; but I haven't seen any attention being paid to the Coal Question. Of course, there has been some expert speculation on how to *get* any coal without twenty dollars, but no one seems to have written anything helpful on what we are going to do with it once we have got it. Or is that just my personal problem?

I have been trying to get coal into a furnace fire box now for about fifteen years, and I should say that my average was about .002, or two pieces of coal to each half ton shoveled. I can get it anywhere else in the cellar—the ash cans, the preserve closet, the boxes behind the furnace, and even back into the bin again. But I can't quite seem to hit the fire box in the furnace.

It may be that there is something wrong with my aim or my eyesight, but I have always had a feeling that the coal itself had something to do with it. I think that my coal man sells me live coal; that is coal which lives and breathes and has a mind of its own. You can't tell me that just ordinary dumb, inanimate coal could act the way mine does!

I would not tell this to many people, because they wouldn't believe me, but I have actually seen pieces of coal which I had successfully tossed into the fire box *turn around and fly back out on to the floor!* Now, you can't fight a thing like that. I have watched coal on a shovel which I was carrying from the bin to the furnace actually set itself in a state of ferment and bound about like corn in a popper in its attempt to get off the shovel and on to the floor. Things of this nature come under the head of the Supernatural. You know that, don't you?

I remember one night back in 1926 when I went down into the cellar to fix the furnace for the night (and what a misleading phrase that "fix the furnace" is! I'd *like* to fix a furnace just once. It wouldn't pull any more of its dirty tricks on me again, I'll tell you. The only way a furnace can be fixed is with nitroglycerin.) Anyway, I went down to give the furnace its head for the night, and to this end I went over to the bin to get the customary three shovelfuls of coal.

The bin was about half full (it then being about the middle of October and the fire about two weeks in operation) and I picked out my favorite shovel—which I had had built like a dredge, with sides which closed up around the coal—and started for the opening. Remember, I could *see* the coal in there.

I dug in the shovel, felt the coal settle on it, and pulled it out. There was no coal there! I then poked down from over the top of the bin with a long poker until I was absolutely sure that I felt great piles of coal descend, all the time saying to myself: "Come, come, Benchley! Pull yourself together! Of course there will be some on the shovel this time." But no! I could not even get those black diamonds out of the bin, much less into the furnace. This was disturbing enough—but wait!

I turned to look at the open door of the fire box into which I had planned to toss at least six or seven pieces, and there, on the floor between the bin and the furnace, was all the coal which hadn't come out on the shovel! It had come out by itself, possibly over my head through the air, and had strewn itself all over the cement in just the position it would have taken anyway, but without a sound! Some of it had even wound its ghostly way over into its favorite nest in the preserve closet and was lying there, looking up at me as if to say: "Beat you to it, old man!" Without another look I

There was all the coal which hadn't come out on the shovel!

turned and fled upstairs, striking my head on the cellar stairs even harder than usual. I know enough not to monkey around with devil's coal.

This experience rather made me afraid to go down cellar again, and I hired a man to do it for me. He, however, seemed to have no trouble, and I used to hear the coal crashing into the furnace below (and what a lovely sound that is, to lie in bed in the morning and hear some other poor sucker downstairs putting on the coal, even if it is only your wife) and my pride became piqued.

If an Italian who had got only an A.B. in a university could get coal into a furnace without spilling it, why couldn't I, with my Ph.D., do it? Or better yet, why couldn't I actually build the fire with my Ph.D.? This was, however, out of the question, as I had lost it that time when the Salvation Army took those old army blankets in which it had been tucked away. But I determined to try my hand at the fire at least once a day, and then, if it didn't work, let Mike go on doing it all the time.

The result of this was that Mike would build the fire in the morning (I chose the evening service for my experiments) and I would put it out at night. Then Mike would build it in the morning again. He finally said that he would have to get more money for tending it just once a day than he did when he tended it twice, as he had more work to do, what with taking out the things that I had put into it the night before (I may not be able to get *coal* into a fire box, but I can get some dandy other things, such as hunks of larva, old bottles, and bits of the cement floor) and then rebuilding the whole business. So I gave it up entirely for the time being. But this winter I had to start in again; for because of the unemployment, Mike has too much work to do on public improvements to bother with us.

I am now thinking of having a furnace built with the coal bin *on top*. Then, when it comes time for me to put on more coal, I can just open a chute and let the stuff dribble down into the fire box at any speed and to any amount that I want.

As for the ashes and clinkers, I shall have a great cavern dug underneath the furnace, with perhaps a small boy who will stand down there with a searchlight and a rifle and who can shoot the clinkers to bits as they stick in the grate.

When the winter is over I can have the house moved right off the cavern and the whole thing dug out.

This, of course, is going to be pretty expensive, and I haven't the slightest idea that it will work. But it will at least restore my self-respect by making it unnecessary for me to go at the thing with that shovel again. And a failure in a rather gigantic effort like that wouldn't be half as humiliating as not being able to get a few pieces of coal into a fire box with my own hands.

*T*ell-*T*ale

*C*lues

UNLESS you are very smart and remember all that was taught you in school about how to cover up your tracks after you have committed a crime, you are going to be surprised at some of the things that I am going to write down for you. And I, in turn, shall be surprised if you read them. The average criminal has no idea how careful he has to be in order to keep on being a criminal and not just an ex-. He may think that he is being careful while he is at work, wearing silk gloves and walking on his ankles and all that, but unless he spends as much time looking around for telltale bits of evidence after he commits the crime as he spent in committing it, then he is leaving himself open for a terrible panning by *some*one, even if it is only the Chief of Police.

For example, on April 7, 1904, the vault in the Lazybones National Bank and Fiduciary Trust Co. of Illville, Illinois, was blown off, and if there had been anything in there worth taking away, it could easily have been done. As it was, the vault contained nothing but a hundred shares of Goldman Sachs, and the robbers, instead of taking these, added two hundred more shares of their own and made their get-away, leaving the bank stuck with three hundred shares instead of one hundred.

Attracted by the oaths of the safe-crackers as they walked down the street, the police rushed first to the Farmers' and Drovers' Bank, then to the First Congregational Church, and then to the Lazybones National where the explosion had taken place. They found that not only had the front been blown off the vault but the handle to the front door of the bank building was gone. It had evidently been pulled off in pique by one of the robbers when he found that the door would not open as easily as he thought it ought to.

After a thorough investigation of the premises, Captain Louis Mildew of the detective force turned to his aid and said, "If we can find the man who has this door knob in his hand, we shall have the man who cracked the safe." A week later a man was picked up in Zanesville who was carrying a door knob which corresponded in every detail with the one missing from the bank building. In spite of the fact that he claimed that it belonged to him and that he was carrying it to ward off rheumatism, he was arrested and later confessed.

Another case where carelessness on the part of the criminal led to his ultimate arrest and embarrassment is found on the records of police in Right Knee, New Jersey. A puddle-worker had been killed in a fight and his assailant had escaped, evidently several days before the crime was discovered (in fact, the evidence pointed to the killer having escaped several days before the murder, which didn't make sense). On looking over the ground where the body was found, the police discovered a man's wooden leg firmly gripped in the teeth of the dead man.

The name of the makers of the wooden leg, the Peter Pan Novelty Co., was also broadcast.

On the fourth day of the search a policeman saw a one-legged man sitting at a bar and, approaching him in a businesslike manner, said, "I represent the Peter Pan Novelty Co. and there is a payment due on an artificial limb bought from us last year. Could you see your way clear to giving us something at this time?"

The one-legged man immediately bridled and said hotly, "I pay you no more on that leg. It came off when I needed it most, and I haven't even been able to find it since. If you wish, I will put this in the form of a letter of complaint to the company."

*A policeman, approaching him, said, "There is a payment due on an
artificial limb bought from us last year."*

"You can put it in the form of testimony before a judge,
buddy," said the policeman, turning back his lapel where
he had forgotten to pin his badge. "Come along with me."

And so, simply through careless haste in getting away
without looking about for incriminating evidence, the man
was caught, and had a pretty rough time convincing the
jury that he had done the killing in self-defense and to save
his sister's honor. It was later found that not only did he
have no sister but that she had no honor.

Perhaps the most famous instance of carelessness was the
discovery of the abductor of the Sacred White Elephant of
Mistick, California. This was an inside job, for the elephant

had been confined in a hut which was several sizes too small for her, making it impossible for anyone to enter from the outside. This much was certain.

The elephant, when it was first discovered in Mistick, had been neither white nor sacred, but was a camp follower of a circus, who had liked the town and stayed behind when the rest moved on. So the town whitewashed her and spread the report about that she was sacred, and used to charge two bits to take a walk around her, once around one way and back around the other.

The man who had turned the trick was a very wily elephant thief who had been in the business a long time but had never worked in white elephants before. He made all provisions for a quick get-away and, before the loss was discovered, had the prize out of town and well on its way down the coast. What he had neglected to do, however, was to brush off the sleeve of his coat, not realizing that, when frightened, a white elephant gives off a fine dusty powder which settles on the nearest objects and marks them as having been near a white elephant. And so it was that, as the crook was walking along a country road leading his ill-gotten gain, he was accosted by a local constable. Stopping Potts (the thief's name was Potts), he said, "What's that white dust on your coat shoulder?"

"I just left my girl," said Potts. "Does your girl wear white elephant powder?" asked the constable, very comical. "That's white elephant powder and it's off that elephant."

"What elephant?" said Potts in surprise, looking behind him. "Oh, *that* elephant?"

The thief tried to escape by hiding behind the beast; but the constable could see his legs and feet from the other side and placed him under arrest.

So you will see that it is the little things that count in successful police evasion, and the sooner our criminals realize this the fewer humiliating arrests there will be.

What
Does Your Boy
Read?

ONE of the reasons children grow up so quickly these days must be that the books which are written for grown-ups are so much more fun to read than the so-called "juvenile literature."

Most of the children's books today are designed to improve the child's mind or inculcate in him a spirit of good clean camel-hunting. Instead of heroes taking pot shots at Indians or hiding gold in caves, we find the continent of South America as the hero of one modern child's book and the man who discovered how to insulate copper wire as the hero of another. What inducement to read is there for a boy who has spent a hard day at school and in the back lot? Now I ask you!

There was such a hue and a cry about the old-fashioned dime novel (which cost a nickel) that no self-respecting parent today would allow his children to have one in the house; and yet Frank and Dick Merriwell, and even Old and Young King Brady, were as highly moral characters as, I venture to say, any of the modern heroes who set out to get specimens of quartz for the Museum and become president of the Interurban Oil Company in the process. Old King Brady did chew a little tobacco now and then, it is true; but most of the dime-novel heroes were models of behavior which many a child of today would do well to follow. I'll bet there are not more than six young men in the country right now as well behaved and noble as Frank Merriwell used to be.

Take the following excerpts (imaginary but typical) from an old-time thriller and a new-fashioned "inspirational" book for children:

"Dick Montague turned and faced the four masked figures who confronted him and Elsie Maxwell as they stood, with their backs to the wall, in Old Indian Meg's cave. His eyes flashed fire as he rolled back one sleeve.

"'Your names are unknown to me,' he said in a calm voice, 'but, unless my eyes deceive me, you are members of the Red Band which has been marauding the country hereabouts. I know you all to be cowards at heart, and although I am not one to pick a fight without justification, I will offer to knock down the first man who dares make a move toward this young lady here!'

"The four blackguards sneered in unison but there was something in Dick Montague's voice which inspired terror in their craven hearts.

"'Come, son, have a cigarette and let's talk it over,' said one of them, taking a step forward.

"Crack! A blow on the face from Dick's fist felled him to the floor of the cave.

"'Get up, you yellow dog!' said Dick (for it was indeed he). 'You know very well that I do not smoke cigarettes, otherwise I should not be able to lead the flying wedge on the Yale football team with such courage.'

"A second member of the gang stepped forward. 'You darned little whelp,' he muttered, 'I'll—'

"But before he could finish his sentence, he, too, lay sprawling on the ground, the victim of a second crashing blow delivered by the young athlete.

"'Get up, you yellow dog,' said Dick, 'and the next time, mind your language when there is a lady about!'"

And now something from the "recommended reading list" for the kiddies, put forward by the National Society for the Drying up of Children's Books:

"Little Sir A. S. Eddington turned to his companions who were clustered about the telescope.

"'It was awfully good of you chaps to ask me here to look

If I were a child I would welcome bedtime.

through your telescope,' he said, wiping off the eyepiece carefully, for you never can tell who has been looking through a telescope before you. 'I wonder if the rest of you boys know that the other name for the Milky Way is the Galaxy.'

"'I knew it, but I had forgotten it,' said H. Spencer Jones, the little boy who was later to become head of the observatory at Edinburgh, but not until he had learned not to forget things.

"'The Galaxy, or Milky Way,' continued little Sir Arthur, 'is perhaps three hundred thousand light-years in diameter. Think of that!'

"'Do we *have* to think of that?' asked happy-go-lucky Dr. Arbuthnot. 'It makes me giddy!'

"There was a general laugh at this, but there were more serious matters to be attended to.

"'The center of the system of globular clusters is in Sagittarius,' continued Sir Arthur—

"'In *what*?' asked someone incredulously.

"'In a group of stars known as Sagittarius,' repeated Sir Arthur impatiently, 'so called because it means "the archer," as this group of stars used to be represented in the old days by the picture of an archer shooting an arrow.'

"'Let's go out and shoot arrows *now*,' suggested Dr. Arbuthnot, and away they all went to shoot arrows."

Now, in this latter form of writing for children there is undoubtedly a great deal of valuable information, but if I were a child (and I sometimes wonder) I would welcome bedtime if that were all I had to sit up for.

When the State Plays Papa

I WILL string along with the radicals on most of their plans for betterment. But there is one item on their schedule which I cannot go for at all. I refer to the raising of children by the state. I don't think that the state quite realizes what it is letting itself in for.

Of course a great many mothers and fathers are unfit to raise children beyond the spitting-up stage, and probably most of the crime and maladjustments of today are due to parents having bought ten-year-old suits for fourteen-year-old boys. But even with the state functioning perfectly I can see nothing but confusion in its attempting to bring up children. I can see nothing but confusion in bringing up children anyway.

Let us suppose, just to drive ourselves crazy, that all children are taken from their parents at the age of two, which is about the age when modern educators begin making children express themselves, whether the children want to express themselves or not. ("Now, Henry Martin Manning, Junior—you go right upstairs and express yourself before you can sit down at the table!") The two-year-olds, on being packed off, bag and baggage, to the State Department of Nurseries and Child Culture, are registered and filed under "Worries." For, with the taking over of the children, the state will have to give up worrying about budgets, deficits, or even counter-revolutions. The kiddies will take up practically all of its time.

In the matter of bathing, for instance. The chairman of the State Bath-Giving Commission will have to be a pretty husky guy who doesn't mind getting a little wet himself. He will not be able to keep his assistants very long unless this is to be a real dictatorship. Giving a three-year-old child a bath is a job that most governments would not want to take on. A peep into the first annual report of the State Bath-Giving Commission will disclose a paragraph like the following:

> Owing to our limited facilities and the difficulty of obtaining competent labor, the department has made a rather poor showing on the year. Baths were attempted on 14,395 children. Baths completed: 75. Injuries to state officials incurred by slipping and striking chin on edge of tub; 8,390. State officials drenched: 14,395. State officials drowned: 11.
>
> If this work is to be continued next year, completely new equipment will have to be bought, including elbow guards and knee pads for the employees, together with a larger and more efficient model face cloth. If the department's appropriation cannot be increased, it is the opinion of the chairman that the project should be abandoned. (As a matter of fact, the chairman is resigning anyway.)

Of course the whole thing will have to be divided up into subcommittees, and there will be work enough for one whole subcommittee in picking up toys and spoons thrown on the floor by children sitting in high chairs. Here is another committee I do not want to be on. *Some*body has got to pick them up, presumably the state. We shall probably get a condition where the official who is supposed to pick up thrown rattles will pass the buck to an underling, who will pass it on to somebody else, with the result that the rattle lies on the floor by the high chair and the child flies into a rage. This is not going to look very pretty for state control, especially if a lot of children fly into rages at once.

This attempt to raise children as a party pledge is going to make the party in power very vulnerable at each election. The anti-Communist candidate, speaking before a group of enraged parents on the street corner, can say:

"And, furthermore, voters of the Eighth Ward, what sort of children are our friends turning out? I will tell you. I had

*"We do not seem to be able to break Marian of the habit
of sticking out her tongue at the officials."*

occasion the other day to invite one of the state's children
into my house for supper, and I may say that I have never
seen a ruder little brat in my whole life. I don't know what
his guardians are thinking of to let him run wild the way he
does. His knuckles were dirty, he didn't answer when spoken
to, and, as I said to my wife, if he were a child of mine I
would have taken him over my knee and given him a good
hiding. If those women at the state nursery would play a
little less bridge and pay more attention to their children—
our children—we wouldn't have so many disrespectful little
hoodlums growing up into unmanageable pests. This condition of things cannot go on a day longer!"

Perhaps it would be just as well to *let* the first Communist
government take the kiddies over and then sit back and wait.
Pretty soon the parents would find themselves being called
to the telephone and asked: "What did you use to do to make
Albert eat his peas?" Or, "We do not seem to be able to
break Marian of the habit of sticking out her tongue at the
officials and saying 'Nya-a-aya!' Did you ever have that
trouble with her?"

As it is, state officials are none too efficient. They don't do very well by the roads, and they made quite a botch of prohibition enforcement. There would be slight chance for graft in the raising of children; in fact, it would cost them a tidy sum in pennies for slot machines and odd dimes to fill up dime banks.

*I*s the

*S*ea *S*erpent a *M*yth

or a *M*ythter?

Now that people are back from the seashore again we can scrutinize those reports on sea serpents! Coming after reports on budgets, taxes, and the increase in pellagra, a good sea-serpent report is a relief. At least there is some ground for argument about a sea serpent.

There was, for instance, the famous serpent seen by the members of the crew of the schooner Mrs. Ella B. Margolies off Gloucester in 1896. I will set down the excerpt from the ship's log for what it is worth (closing price .003):

"On Board Mrs. Ella B. Margolies. August 6, 1896. Lat. 24° 57′ S., long. 16 ft. E. . . . Brooklyn-8; St. Louis-4. . . . Am. T. & T. 20½.

"In the 4 to 6 watch, at about 5 o'clock, we observed a most remarkable fish on our lee quarter, crossing the stern in a S.W. direction. The appearance of the head, which with the back fin (or upper leg) was the only portion of the animal visible, was something similar to that of a rabbit, only without the ears. It (the animal) pursued a steady undeviating course, keeping its head horizontal with the surface of the water except when it turned to look backward as if it were flirting with something.

"Once a small pennant was raised just above where the tail should be, a pennant which, according to the code of the sea, signified 'Owner on Board.'"

This same animal was seen from points along the shore at

Gloucester and Bass Rock, and officials of the Odd Creatures Society took the trouble to investigate. The answers given by Roger Bivalve, a fisherman living in a lobster trap on Point Pixie, are representative as well as enlightening.

Q. When did you first see the animal?

A. I should say shortly after falling down on the rocks in front of my place.

Q. At what distance?

A. Once it was in my lap. Other times about fifty yards out.

Q. What was its general appearance?

A. Something awful.

Q. Did it appear jointed or serpentine?

A. Serpentine, by all means.

Q. Describe its eyes and mouth.

A. Well, its eyes were beautiful. I thought for a while that I was in love with it. Its mouth was more mocking than anything, which gave me the tip-off.

Q. Had it fins or legs, and where?

A. Do I have to answer that?

Q. Did it make any sound or noise?

A. I should say it was more of a cackle, or perhaps a laugh. I know I didn't like it.

Q. Do you drink?

A. Only medicinally, and then never after I fall over.

It is too bad that there should be this suspicion of excess drinking attached to reports of sea serpents, because I myself have a story which might help solve a great many problems in marine mystery, but I fear the effect it might have on my children's opinion of me.

Oh, well, I might as well get it off my chest! . . . I am not a drinking man by nature, and although on this particular day I had rubbed a little alcohol into my hair to keep the flies away, I have every reason to believe that I was in full possession of my senses. (I don't suppose that I can say *full* possession, for I have three more payments to make before they are really mine.) I had been talking to an old friend whom I hadn't seen for years, and the next time we looked at

the clock it was Friday; so I said: "Well, Harry, what do you say we call it a week and knock off?" Harry was agreeable, so we went and bought two hats to put on so that we wouldn't have to go home bareheaded.

I know that this sounds fishy, but just as sure as I am standing here at this minute, I looked down the length of the hat store, and there, right by the little door where the clerks went in and out, something caught my eye—no mean trick in itself, as my eye was not in a roving mood right then, as I was concentrating on a brown fedora which I fortunately did not buy. It was as if something with a long tail had just disappeared around the corner of the door.

I thought nothing of it at first, thinking that it was probably a salesman who had a long tail and who was going about his business. But the more I thought it over the stranger it seemed to me that I had not noticed a salesman with a long tail before, as we had been in the shop several hours by this time.

So I excused myself politely and tiptoed down to the door where I had seen the disappearing object. It was quite a long walk, as I got into another store by mistake and had to inquire my way back, but soon I reached the rear of the original hat store and looked out into the workroom. There, stretched across an ironing board where they had been reblocking old derbies, I saw a sight which made my blood run cold.

Beginning at one end of the ironing board and stretching across it and off the other end into the window—

I guess that I was right in the first place. I never should have begun to tell it. You wouldn't understand!

A CATALOG OF SELECTED
DOVER BOOKS
IN ALL FIELDS OF INTEREST

A CATALOG OF SELECTED DOVER BOOKS IN ALL FIELDS OF INTEREST

DRAWINGS OF REMBRANDT, edited by Seymour Slive. Updated Lippmann, Hofstede de Groot edition, with definitive scholarly apparatus. All portraits, biblical sketches, landscapes, nudes. Oriental figures, classical studies, together with selection of work by followers. 550 illustrations. Total of 630pp. 9⅛ × 12¼.
21485-0, 21486-9 Pa., Two-vol. set $25.00

GHOST AND HORROR STORIES OF AMBROSE BIERCE, Ambrose Bierce. 24 tales vividly imagined, strangely prophetic, and decades ahead of their time in technical skill: "The Damned Thing," "An Inhabitant of Carcosa," "The Eyes of the Panther," "Moxon's Master," and 20 more. 199pp. 5⅜ × 8½. 20767-6 Pa. $3.95

ETHICAL WRITINGS OF MAIMONIDES, Maimonides. Most significant ethical works of great medieval sage, newly translated for utmost precision, readability. Laws Concerning Character Traits, Eight Chapters, more. 192pp. 5⅜ × 8½.
24522-5 Pa. $4.50

THE EXPLORATION OF THE COLORADO RIVER AND ITS CANYONS, J. W. Powell. Full text of Powell's 1,000-mile expedition down the fabled Colorado in 1869. Superb account of terrain, geology, vegetation, Indians, famine, mutiny, treacherous rapids, mighty canyons, during exploration of last unknown part of continental U.S. 400pp. 5⅜ × 8½. 20094-9 Pa. $6.95

HISTORY OF PHILOSOPHY, Julián Marías. Clearest one-volume history on the market. Every major philosopher and dozens of others, to Existentialism and later. 505pp. 5⅜ × 8½. 21739-6 Pa. $8.50

ALL ABOUT LIGHTNING, Martin A. Uman. Highly readable non-technical survey of nature and causes of lightning, thunderstorms, ball lightning, St. Elmo's Fire, much more. Illustrated. 192pp. 5⅜ × 8½. 25237-X Pa. $5.95

SAILING ALONE AROUND THE WORLD, Captain Joshua Slocum. First man to sail around the world, alone, in small boat. One of great feats of seamanship told in delightful manner. 67 illustrations. 294pp. 5⅜ × 8½. 20326-3 Pa. $4.95

LETTERS AND NOTES ON THE MANNERS, CUSTOMS AND CONDITIONS OF THE NORTH AMERICAN INDIANS, George Catlin. Classic account of life among Plains Indians: ceremonies, hunt, warfare, etc. 312 plates. 572pp. of text. 6⅛ × 9¼. 22118-0, 22119-9 Pa. Two-vol. set $15.90

ALASKA: The Harriman Expedition, 1899, John Burroughs, John Muir, et al. Informative, engrossing accounts of two-month, 9,000-mile expedition. Native peoples, wildlife, forests, geography, salmon industry, glaciers, more. Profusely illustrated. 240 black-and-white line drawings. 124 black-and-white photographs. 3 maps. Index. 576pp. 5⅜ × 8½. 25109-8 Pa. $11.95

THE BOOK OF BEASTS: Being a Translation from a Latin Bestiary of the Twelfth Century, T. H. White. Wonderful catalog real and fanciful beasts: manticore, griffin, phoenix, amphivius, jaculus, many more. White's witty erudite commentary on scientific, historical aspects. Fascinating glimpse of medieval mind. Illustrated. 296pp. 5⅜ × 8¼. (Available in U.S. only) 24609-4 Pa. $5.95

FRANK LLOYD WRIGHT: ARCHITECTURE AND NATURE With 160 Illustrations, Donald Hoffmann. Profusely illustrated study of influence of nature—especially prairie—on Wright's designs for Fallingwater, Robie House, Guggenheim Museum, other masterpieces. 96pp. 9¼ × 10¾. 25098-9 Pa. $7.95

FRANK LLOYD WRIGHT'S FALLINGWATER, Donald Hoffmann. Wright's famous waterfall house: planning and construction of organic idea. History of site, owners, Wright's personal involvement. Photographs of various stages of building. Preface by Edgar Kaufmann, Jr. 100 illustrations. 112pp. 9¼ × 10.
23671-4 Pa. $7.95

YEARS WITH FRANK LLOYD WRIGHT: Apprentice to Genius, Edgar Tafel. Insightful memoir by a former apprentice presents a revealing portrait of Wright the man, the inspired teacher, the greatest American architect. 372 black-and-white illustrations. Preface. Index. vi + 228pp. 8¼ × 11. 24801-1 Pa. $9.95

THE STORY OF KING ARTHUR AND HIS KNIGHTS, Howard Pyle. Enchanting version of King Arthur fable has delighted generations with imaginative narratives of exciting adventures and unforgettable illustrations by the author. 41 illustrations. xviii + 313pp. 6⅛ × 9¼. 21445-1 Pa. $6.50

THE GODS OF THE EGYPTIANS, E. A. Wallis Budge. Thorough coverage of numerous gods of ancient Egypt by foremost Egyptologist. Information on evolution of cults, rites and gods; the cult of Osiris; the Book of the Dead and its rites; the sacred animals and birds; Heaven and Hell; and more. 956pp. 6⅛ × 9¼.
22055-9, 22056-7 Pa., Two-vol. set $20.00

A THEOLOGICO-POLITICAL TREATISE, Benedict Spinoza. Also contains unfinished *Political Treatise*. Great classic on religious liberty, theory of government on common consent. R. Elwes translation. Total of 421pp. 5⅜ × 8½.
20249-6 Pa. $6.95

INCIDENTS OF TRAVEL IN CENTRAL AMERICA, CHIAPAS, AND YUCATAN, John L. Stephens. Almost single-handed discovery of Maya culture; exploration of ruined cities, monuments, temples; customs of Indians. 115 drawings. 892pp. 5⅜ × 8½. 22404-X, 22405-8 Pa., Two-vol. set $15.90

LOS CAPRICHOS, Francisco Goya. 80 plates of wild, grotesque monsters and caricatures. Prado manuscript included. 183pp. 6⅝ × 9⅝. 22384-1 Pa. $4.95

AUTOBIOGRAPHY: The Story of My Experiments with Truth, Mohandas K. Gandhi. Not hagiography, but Gandhi in his own words. Boyhood, legal studies, purification, the growth of the Satyagraha (nonviolent protest) movement. Critical, inspiring work of the man who freed India. 480pp. 5⅜ × 8½. (Available in U.S. only)
24593-4 Pa. $6.95

ILLUSTRATED DICTIONARY OF HISTORIC ARCHITECTURE, edited by Cyril M. Harris. Extraordinary compendium of clear, concise definitions for over 5,000 important architectural terms complemented by over 2,000 line drawings. Covers full spectrum of architecture from ancient ruins to 20th-century Modernism. Preface. 592pp. 7½ × 9⅝. 24444-X Pa. $14.95

THE NIGHT BEFORE CHRISTMAS, Clement Moore. Full text, and woodcuts from original 1848 book. Also critical, historical material. 19 illustrations. 40pp. 4⅝ × 6. 22797-9 Pa. $2.25

THE LESSON OF JAPANESE ARCHITECTURE: 165 Photographs, Jiro Harada. Memorable gallery of 165 photographs taken in the 1930's of exquisite Japanese homes of the well-to-do and historic buildings. 13 line diagrams. 192pp. 8⅜ × 11¼. 24778-3 Pa. $8.95

THE AUTOBIOGRAPHY OF CHARLES DARWIN AND SELECTED LETTERS, edited by Francis Darwin. The fascinating life of eccentric genius composed of an intimate memoir by Darwin (intended for his children); commentary by his son, Francis; hundreds of fragments from notebooks, journals, papers; and letters to and from Lyell, Hooker, Huxley, Wallace and Henslow. xi + 365pp. 5⅜ × 8. 20479-0 Pa. $6.95

WONDERS OF THE SKY: Observing Rainbows, Comets, Eclipses, the Stars and Other Phenomena, Fred Schaaf. Charming, easy-to-read poetic guide to all manner of celestial events visible to the naked eye. Mock suns, glories, Belt of Venus, more. Illustrated. 299pp. 5¼ × 8¼. 24402-4 Pa. $7.95

BURNHAM'S CELESTIAL HANDBOOK, Robert Burnham, Jr. Thorough guide to the stars beyond our solar system. Exhaustive treatment. Alphabetical by constellation: Andromeda to Cetus in Vol. 1; Chamaeleon to Orion in Vol. 2; and Pavo to Vulpecula in Vol. 3. Hundreds of illustrations. Index in Vol. 3. 2,000pp. 6⅛ × 9¼. 23567-X, 23568-8, 23673-0 Pa., Three-vol. set $38.85

STAR NAMES: Their Lore and Meaning, Richard Hinckley Allen. Fascinating history of names various cultures have given to constellations and literary and folkloristic uses that have been made of stars. Indexes to subjects. Arabic and Greek names. Biblical references. Bibliography. 563pp. 5⅜ × 8½. 21079-0 Pa. $7.95

THIRTY YEARS THAT SHOOK PHYSICS: The Story of Quantum Theory, George Gamow. Lucid, accessible introduction to influential theory of energy and matter. Careful explanations of Dirac's anti-particles, Bohr's model of the atom, much more. 12 plates. Numerous drawings. 240pp. 5⅜ × 8½. 24895-X Pa. $4.95

CHINESE DOMESTIC FURNITURE IN PHOTOGRAPHS AND MEASURED DRAWINGS, Gustav Ecke. A rare volume, now affordably priced for antique collectors, furniture buffs and art historians. Detailed review of styles ranging from early Shang to late Ming. Unabridged republication. 161 black-and-white drawings, photos. Total of 224pp. 8⅜ × 11¼. (Available in U.S. only) 25171-3 Pa. $12.95

VINCENT VAN GOGH: A Biography, Julius Meier-Graefe. Dynamic, penetrating study of artist's life, relationship with brother, Theo, painting techniques, travels, more. Readable, engrossing. 160pp. 5⅜ × 8½. (Available in U.S. only) 25253-1 Pa. $3.95

HOW TO WRITE, Gertrude Stein. Gertrude Stein claimed anyone could understand her unconventional writing—here are clues to help. Fascinating improvisations, language experiments, explanations illuminate Stein's craft and the art of writing. Total of 414pp. 4⅜ × 6⅜. 23144-5 Pa. $5.95

ADVENTURES AT SEA IN THE GREAT AGE OF SAIL: Five Firsthand Narratives, edited by Elliot Snow. Rare true accounts of exploration, whaling, shipwreck, fierce natives, trade, shipboard life, more. 33 illustrations. Introduction. 353pp. 5⅜ × 8½. 25177-2 Pa. $7.95

THE HERBAL OR GENERAL HISTORY OF PLANTS, John Gerard. Classic descriptions of about 2,850 plants—with over 2,700 illustrations—includes Latin and English names, physical descriptions, varieties, time and place of growth, more. 2,706 illustrations. xlv + 1,678pp. 8½ × 12¼. 23147-X Cloth. $75.00

DOROTHY AND THE WIZARD IN OZ, L. Frank Baum. Dorothy and the Wizard visit the center of the Earth, where people are vegetables, glass houses grow and Oz characters reappear. Classic sequel to *Wizard of Oz*. 256pp. 5⅜ × 8. 24714-7 Pa. $4.95

SONGS OF EXPERIENCE: Facsimile Reproduction with 26 Plates in Full Color, William Blake. This facsimile of Blake's original "Illuminated Book" reproduces 26 full-color plates from a rare 1826 edition. Includes "The Tyger," "London," "Holy Thursday," and other immortal poems. 26 color plates. Printed text of poems. 48pp. 5¼ × 7. 24636-1 Pa. $3.50

SONGS OF INNOCENCE, William Blake. The first and most popular of Blake's famous "Illuminated Books," in a facsimile edition reproducing all 31 brightly colored plates. Additional printed text of each poem. 64pp. 5¼ × 7. 22764-2 Pa. $3.50

PRECIOUS STONES, Max Bauer. Classic, thorough study of diamonds, rubies, emeralds, garnets, etc.: physical character, occurrence, properties, use, similar topics. 20 plates, 8 in color. 94 figures. 659pp. 6⅛ × 9¼. 21910-0, 21911-9 Pa., Two-vol. set $15.90

ENCYCLOPEDIA OF VICTORIAN NEEDLEWORK, S. F. A. Caulfeild and Blanche Saward. Full, precise descriptions of stitches, techniques for dozens of needlecrafts—most exhaustive reference of its kind. Over 800 figures. Total of 679pp. 8⅛ × 11. Two volumes. Vol. 1 22800-2 Pa. $11.95
Vol. 2 22801-0 Pa. $11.95

THE MARVELOUS LAND OF OZ, L. Frank Baum. Second Oz book, the Scarecrow and Tin Woodman are back with hero named Tip, Oz magic. 136 illustrations. 287pp. 5⅜ × 8½. 20692-0 Pa. $5.95

WILD FOWL DECOYS, Joel Barber. Basic book on the subject, by foremost authority and collector. Reveals history of decoy making and rigging, place in American culture, different kinds of decoys, how to make them, and how to use them. 140 plates. 156pp. 7⅞ × 10¾. 20011-6 Pa. $8.95

HISTORY OF LACE, Mrs. Bury Palliser. Definitive, profusely illustrated chronicle of lace from earliest times to late 19th century. Laces of Italy, Greece, England, France, Belgium, etc. Landmark of needlework scholarship. 266 illustrations. 672pp. 6⅛ × 9¼. 24742-2 Pa. $14.95

ILLUSTRATED GUIDE TO SHAKER FURNITURE, Robert Meader. All furniture and appurtenances, with much on unknown local styles. 235 photos. 146pp. 9 × 12. 22819-3 Pa. $7.95

WHALE SHIPS AND WHALING: A Pictorial Survey, George Francis Dow. Over 200 vintage engravings, drawings, photographs of barks, brigs, cutters, other vessels. Also harpoons, lances, whaling guns, many other artifacts. Comprehensive text by foremost authority. 207 black-and-white illustrations. 288pp. 6 × 9. 24808-9 Pa. $8.95

THE BERTRAMS, Anthony Trollope. Powerful portrayal of blind self-will and thwarted ambition includes one of Trollope's most heartrending love stories. 497pp. 5⅜ × 8½. 25119-5 Pa. $8.95

ADVENTURES WITH A HAND LENS, Richard Headstrom. Clearly written guide to observing and studying flowers and grasses, fish scales, moth and insect wings, egg cases, buds, feathers, seeds, leaf scars, moss, molds, ferns, common crystals, etc.—all with an ordinary, inexpensive magnifying glass. 209 exact line drawings aid in your discoveries. 220pp. 5⅜ × 8½. 23330-8 Pa. $3.95

RODIN ON ART AND ARTISTS, Auguste Rodin. Great sculptor's candid, wide-ranging comments on meaning of art; great artists; relation of sculpture to poetry, painting, music; philosophy of life, more. 76 superb black-and-white illustrations of Rodin's sculpture, drawings and prints. 119pp. 8⅜ × 11¼. 24487-3 Pa. $6.95

FIFTY CLASSIC FRENCH FILMS, 1912–1982: A Pictorial Record, Anthony Slide. Memorable stills from Grand Illusion, Beauty and the Beast, Hiroshima, Mon Amour, many more. Credits, plot synopses, reviews, etc. 160pp. 8¼ × 11. 25256-6 Pa. $11.95

THE PRINCIPLES OF PSYCHOLOGY, William James. Famous long course complete, unabridged. Stream of thought, time perception, memory, experimental methods; great work decades ahead of its time. 94 figures. 1,391pp. 5⅜ × 8½. 20381-6, 20382-4 Pa., Two-vol. set $19.90

BODIES IN A BOOKSHOP, R. T. Campbell. Challenging mystery of blackmail and murder with ingenious plot and superbly drawn characters. In the best tradition of British suspense fiction. 192pp. 5⅜ × 8½. 24720-1 Pa. $3.95

CALLAS: PORTRAIT OF A PRIMA DONNA, George Jellinek. Renowned commentator on the musical scene chronicles incredible career and life of the most controversial, fascinating, influential operatic personality of our time. 64 black-and-white photographs. 416pp. 5⅜ × 8¼. 25047-4 Pa. $7.95

GEOMETRY, RELATIVITY AND THE FOURTH DIMENSION, Rudolph Rucker. Exposition of fourth dimension, concepts of relativity as Flatland characters continue adventures. Popular, easily followed yet accurate, profound. 141 illustrations. 133pp. 5⅜ × 8½. 23400-2 Pa. $3.95

HOUSEHOLD STORIES BY THE BROTHERS GRIMM, with pictures by Walter Crane. 53 classic stories—Rumpelstiltskin, Rapunzel, Hansel and Gretel, the Fisherman and his Wife, Snow White, Tom Thumb, Sleeping Beauty, Cinderella, and so much more—lavishly illustrated with original 19th century drawings. 114 illustrations. x + 269pp. 5⅜ × 8½. 21080-4 Pa. $4.50

SUNDIALS, Albert Waugh. Far and away the best, most thorough coverage of ideas, mathematics concerned, types, construction, adjusting anywhere. Over 100 illustrations. 230pp. 5⅜ × 8½. 22947-5 Pa. $4.50

PICTURE HISTORY OF THE NORMANDIE: With 190 Illustrations, Frank O. Braynard. Full story of legendary French ocean liner: Art Deco interiors, design innovations, furnishings, celebrities, maiden voyage, tragic fire, much more. Extensive text. 144pp. 8⅞ × 11¼. 25257-4 Pa. $9.95

THE FIRST AMERICAN COOKBOOK: A Facsimile of "American Cookery," 1796, Amelia Simmons. Facsimile of the first American-written cookbook published in the United States contains authentic recipes for colonial favorites—pumpkin pudding, winter squash pudding, spruce beer, Indian slapjacks, and more. Introductory Essay and Glossary of colonial cooking terms. 80pp. 5⅜ × 8½. 24710-4 Pa. $3.50

101 PUZZLES IN THOUGHT AND LOGIC, C. R. Wylie, Jr. Solve murders and robberies, find out which fishermen are liars, how a blind man could possibly identify a color—purely by your own reasoning! 107pp. 5⅜ × 8½. 20367-0 Pa. $2.50

THE BOOK OF WORLD-FAMOUS MUSIC—CLASSICAL, POPULAR AND FOLK, James J. Fuld. Revised and enlarged republication of landmark work in musico-bibliography. Full information about nearly 1,000 songs and compositions including first lines of music and lyrics. New supplement. Index. 800pp. 5⅜ × 8½. 24857-7 Pa. $14.95

ANTHROPOLOGY AND MODERN LIFE, Franz Boas. Great anthropologist's classic treatise on race and culture. Introduction by Ruth Bunzel. Only inexpensive paperback edition. 255pp. 5⅜ × 8½. 25245-0 Pa. $5.95

THE TALE OF PETER RABBIT, Beatrix Potter. The inimitable Peter's terrifying adventure in Mr. McGregor's garden, with all 27 wonderful, full-color Potter illustrations. 55pp. 4¼ × 5½. (Available in U.S. only) 22827-4 Pa. $1.75

THREE PROPHETIC SCIENCE FICTION NOVELS, H. G. Wells. *When the Sleeper Wakes, A Story of the Days to Come* and *The Time Machine* (full version). 335pp. 5⅜ × 8½. (Available in U.S. only) 20605-X Pa. $5.95

APICIUS COOKERY AND DINING IN IMPERIAL ROME, edited and translated by Joseph Dommers Vehling. Oldest known cookbook in existence offers readers a clear picture of what foods Romans ate, how they prepared them, etc. 49 illustrations. 301pp. 6⅛ × 9¼. 23563-7 Pa. $6.50

SHAKESPEARE LEXICON AND QUOTATION DICTIONARY, Alexander Schmidt. Full definitions, locations, shades of meaning of every word in plays and poems. More than 50,000 exact quotations. 1,485pp. 6½ × 9¼. 22726-X, 22727-8 Pa., Two-vol. set $27.90

THE WORLD'S GREAT SPEECHES, edited by Lewis Copeland and Lawrence W. Lamm. Vast collection of 278 speeches from Greeks to 1970. Powerful and effective models; unique look at history. 842pp. 5⅜ × 8½. 20468-5 Pa. $11.95

THE BLUE FAIRY BOOK, Andrew Lang. The first, most famous collection, with many familiar tales: Little Red Riding Hood, Aladdin and the Wonderful Lamp, Puss in Boots, Sleeping Beauty, Hansel and Gretel, Rumpelstiltskin; 37 in all. 138 illustrations. 390pp. 5⅜ × 8½. 21437-0 Pa. $5.95

THE STORY OF THE CHAMPIONS OF THE ROUND TABLE, Howard Pyle. Sir Launcelot, Sir Tristram and Sir Percival in spirited adventures of love and triumph retold in Pyle's inimitable style. 50 drawings, 31 full-page. xviii + 329pp. 6½ × 9¼. 21883-X Pa. $6.95

AUDUBON AND HIS JOURNALS, Maria Audubon. Unmatched two-volume portrait of the great artist, naturalist and author contains his journals, an excellent biography by his granddaughter, expert annotations by the noted ornithologist, Dr. Elliott Coues, and 37 superb illustrations. Total of 1,200pp. 5⅜ × 8.
Vol. I 25143-8 Pa. $8.95
Vol. II 25144-6 Pa. $8.95

GREAT DINOSAUR HUNTERS AND THEIR DISCOVERIES, Edwin H. Colbert. Fascinating, lavishly illustrated chronicle of dinosaur research, 1820's to 1960. Achievements of Cope, Marsh, Brown, Buckland, Mantell, Huxley, many others. 384pp. 5¼ × 8¼. 24701-5 Pa. $6.95

THE TASTEMAKERS, Russell Lynes. Informal, illustrated social history of American taste 1850's–1950's. First popularized categories Highbrow, Lowbrow, Middlebrow. 129 illustrations. New (1979) afterword. 384pp. 6 × 9.
23993-4 Pa. $6.95

DOUBLE CROSS PURPOSES, Ronald A. Knox. A treasure hunt in the Scottish Highlands, an old map, unidentified corpse, surprise discoveries keep reader guessing in this cleverly intricate tale of financial skullduggery. 2 black-and-white maps. 320pp. 5⅜ × 8½. (Available in U.S. only) 25032-6 Pa. $5.95

AUTHENTIC VICTORIAN DECORATION AND ORNAMENTATION IN FULL COLOR: 46 Plates from "Studies in Design," Christopher Dresser. Superb full-color lithographs reproduced from rare original portfolio of a major Victorian designer. 48pp. 9¼ × 12¼. 25083-0 Pa. $7.95

PRIMITIVE ART, Franz Boas. Remains the best text ever prepared on subject, thoroughly discussing Indian, African, Asian, Australian, and, especially, Northern American primitive art. Over 950 illustrations show ceramics, masks, totem poles, weapons, textiles, paintings, much more. 376pp. 5⅜ × 8. 20025-6 Pa. $6.95

SIDELIGHTS ON RELATIVITY, Albert Einstein. Unabridged republication of two lectures delivered by the great physicist in 1920–21. *Ether and Relativity* and *Geometry and Experience*. Elegant ideas in non-mathematical form, accessible to intelligent layman. vi + 56pp. 5⅜ × 8½. 24511-X Pa. $2.95

THE WIT AND HUMOR OF OSCAR WILDE, edited by Alvin Redman. More than 1,000 ripostes, paradoxes, wisecracks: Work is the curse of the drinking classes, I can resist everything except temptation, etc. 258pp. 5⅜ × 8½. 20602-5 Pa. $4.50

ADVENTURES WITH A MICROSCOPE, Richard Headstrom. 59 adventures with clothing fibers, protozoa, ferns and lichens, roots and leaves, much more. 142 illustrations. 232pp. 5⅜ × 8½. 23471-1 Pa. $3.95

CATALOG OF DOVER BOOKS

PLANTS OF THE BIBLE, Harold N. Moldenke and Alma L. Moldenke. Standard reference to all 230 plants mentioned in Scriptures. Latin name, biblical reference, uses, modern identity, much more. Unsurpassed encyclopedic resource for scholars, botanists, nature lovers, students of Bible. Bibliography. Indexes. 123 black-and-white illustrations. 384pp. 6 × 9. 25069-5 Pa. $8.95

FAMOUS AMERICAN WOMEN: A Biographical Dictionary from Colonial Times to the Present, Robert McHenry, ed. From Pocahontas to Rosa Parks, 1,035 distinguished American women documented in separate biographical entries. Accurate, up-to-date data, numerous categories, spans 400 years. Indices. 493pp. 6½ × 9¼. 24523-3 Pa. $9.95

THE FABULOUS INTERIORS OF THE GREAT OCEAN LINERS IN HISTORIC PHOTOGRAPHS, William H. Miller, Jr. Some 200 superb photographs capture exquisite interiors of world's great "floating palaces"—1890's to 1980's: Titanic, Ile de France, Queen Elizabeth, United States, Europa, more. Approx. 200 black-and-white photographs. Captions. Text. Introduction. 160pp. 8⅜ × 11¾. 24756-2 Pa. $9.95

THE GREAT LUXURY LINERS, 1927-1954: A Photographic Record, William H. Miller, Jr. Nostalgic tribute to heyday of ocean liners. 186 photos of Ile de France, Normandie, Leviathan, Queen Elizabeth, United States, many others. Interior and exterior views. Introduction. Captions. 160pp. 9 × 12. 24056-8 Pa. $9.95

A NATURAL HISTORY OF THE DUCKS, John Charles Phillips. Great landmark of ornithology offers complete detailed coverage of nearly 200 species and subspecies of ducks: gadwall, sheldrake, merganser, pintail, many more. 74 full-color plates, 102 black-and-white. Bibliography. Total of 1,920pp. 8⅜ × 11¼. 25141-1, 25142-X Cloth. Two-vol. set $100.00

THE SEAWEED HANDBOOK: An Illustrated Guide to Seaweeds from North Carolina to Canada, Thomas F. Lee. Concise reference covers 78 species. Scientific and common names, habitat, distribution, more. Finding keys for easy identification. 224pp. 5⅜ × 8½. 25215-9 Pa. $5.95

THE TEN BOOKS OF ARCHITECTURE: The 1755 Leoni Edition, Leon Battista Alberti. Rare classic helped introduce the glories of ancient architecture to the Renaissance. 68 black-and-white plates. 336pp. 8⅜ × 11¼. 25239-6 Pa. $14.95

MISS MACKENZIE, Anthony Trollope. Minor masterpieces by Victorian master unmasks many truths about life in 19th-century England. First inexpensive edition in years. 392pp. 5⅜ × 8½. 25201-9 Pa. $7.95

THE RIME OF THE ANCIENT MARINER, Gustave Doré, Samuel Taylor Coleridge. Dramatic engravings considered by many to be his greatest work. The terrifying space of the open sea, the storms and whirlpools of an unknown ocean, the ice of Antarctica, more—all rendered in a powerful, chilling manner. Full text. 38 plates. 77pp. 9¼ × 12. 22305-1 Pa. $4.95

THE EXPEDITIONS OF ZEBULON MONTGOMERY PIKE, Zebulon Montgomery Pike. Fascinating first-hand accounts (1805-6) of exploration of Mississippi River, Indian wars, capture by Spanish dragoons, much more. 1,088pp. 5⅜ × 8½. 25254-X, 25255-8 Pa. Two-vol. set $23.90

A CONCISE HISTORY OF PHOTOGRAPHY: Third Revised Edition, Helmut Gernsheim. Best one-volume history—camera obscura, photochemistry, daguerreotypes, evolution of cameras, film, more. Also artistic aspects—landscape, portraits, fine art, etc. 281 black-and-white photographs. 26 in color. 176pp. 8⅜ × 11¼. 25128-4 Pa. $12.95

THE DORÉ BIBLE ILLUSTRATIONS, Gustave Doré. 241 detailed plates from the Bible: the Creation scenes, Adam and Eve, Flood, Babylon, battle sequences, life of Jesus, etc. Each plate is accompanied by the verses from the King James version of the Bible. 241pp. 9 × 12. 23004-X Pa. $8.95

HUGGER-MUGGER IN THE LOUVRE, Elliot Paul. Second Homer Evans mystery-comedy. Theft at the Louvre involves sleuth in hilarious, madcap caper. "A knockout."—Books. 336pp. 5⅜ × 8½. 25185-3 Pa. $5.95

FLATLAND, E. A. Abbott. Intriguing and enormously popular science-fiction classic explores the complexities of trying to survive as a two-dimensional being in a three-dimensional world. Amusingly illustrated by the author. 16 illustrations. 103pp. 5⅜ × 8½. 20001-9 Pa. $2.25

THE HISTORY OF THE LEWIS AND CLARK EXPEDITION, Meriwether Lewis and William Clark, edited by Elliott Coues. Classic edition of Lewis and Clark's day-by-day journals that later became the basis for U.S. claims to Oregon and the West. Accurate and invaluable geographical, botanical, biological, meteorological and anthropological material. Total of 1,508pp. 5⅜ × 8½.
21268-8, 21269-6, 21270-X Pa. Three-vol. set $25.50

LANGUAGE, TRUTH AND LOGIC, Alfred J. Ayer. Famous, clear introduction to Vienna, Cambridge schools of Logical Positivism. Role of philosophy, elimination of metaphysics, nature of analysis, etc. 160pp. 5⅜ × 8½. (Available in U.S. and Canada only) 20010-8 Pa. $2.95

MATHEMATICS FOR THE NONMATHEMATICIAN, Morris Kline. Detailed, college-level treatment of mathematics in cultural and historical context, with numerous exercises. For liberal arts students. Preface. Recommended Reading Lists. Tables. Index. Numerous black-and-white figures. xvi + 641pp. 5⅜ × 8½.
24823-2 Pa. $11.95

28 SCIENCE FICTION STORIES, H. G. Wells. Novels, *Star Begotten* and *Men Like Gods,* plus 26 short stories: "Empire of the Ants," "A Story of the Stone Age," "The Stolen Bacillus," "In the Abyss," etc. 915pp. 5⅜ × 8½. (Available in U.S. only)
20265-8 Cloth. $10.95

HANDBOOK OF PICTORIAL SYMBOLS, Rudolph Modley. 3,250 signs and symbols, many systems in full; official or heavy commercial use. Arranged by subject. Most in Pictorial Archive series. 143pp. 8⅛ × 11. 23357-X Pa. $5.95

INCIDENTS OF TRAVEL IN YUCATAN, John L. Stephens. Classic (1843) exploration of jungles of Yucatan, looking for evidences of Maya civilization. Travel adventures, Mexican and Indian culture, etc. Total of 669pp. 5⅜ × 8½.
20926-1, 20927-X Pa., Two-vol. set $9.90

CATALOG OF DOVER BOOKS

DEGAS: An Intimate Portrait, Ambroise Vollard. Charming, anecdotal memoir by famous art dealer of one of the greatest 19th-century French painters. 14 black-and-white illustrations. Introduction by Harold L. Van Doren. 96pp. 5⅜ × 8½.
25131-4 Pa. $3.95

PERSONAL NARRATIVE OF A PILGRIMAGE TO ALMANDINAH AND MECCAH, Richard Burton. Great travel classic by remarkably colorful personality. Burton, disguised as a Moroccan, visited sacred shrines of Islam, narrowly escaping death. 47 illustrations. 959pp. 5⅜ × 8½. 21217-3, 21218-1 Pa., Two-vol. set $19.90

PHRASE AND WORD ORIGINS, A. H. Holt. Entertaining, reliable, modern study of more than 1,200 colorful words, phrases, origins and histories. Much unexpected information. 254pp. 5⅜ × 8½. 20758-7 Pa $4.95

THE RED THUMB MARK, R. Austin Freeman. In this first Dr. Thorndyke case, the great scientific detective draws fascinating conclusions from the nature of a single fingerprint. Exciting story, authentic science. 320pp. 5⅜ × 8½. (Available in U.S. only) 25210-8 Pa $5.95

AN EGYPTIAN HIEROGLYPHIC DICTIONARY, E. A. Wallis Budge. Monumental work containing about 25,000 words or terms that occur in texts ranging from 3000 B.C. to 600 A.D. Each entry consists of a transliteration of the word, the word in hieroglyphs, and the meaning in English. 1,314pp. 6⅜ × 10.
23615-3, 23616-1 Pa., Two-vol. set $27.90

THE COMPLEAT STRATEGYST: Being a Primer on the Theory of Games of Strategy, J. D. Williams. Highly entertaining classic describes, with many illustrated examples, how to select best strategies in conflict situations. Prefaces. Appendices. xvi + 268pp. 5⅜ × 8½. 25101-2 Pa. $5.95

THE ROAD TO OZ, L. Frank Baum. Dorothy meets the Shaggy Man, little Button-Bright and the Rainbow's beautiful daughter in this delightful trip to the magical Land of Oz. 272pp. 5⅜ × 8. 25208-6 Pa. $4.95

POINT AND LINE TO PLANE, Wassily Kandinsky. Seminal exposition of role of point, line, other elements in non-objective painting. Essential to understanding 20th-century art. 127 illustrations. 192pp. 6½ × 9¼. 23808-3 Pa. $4.50

LADY ANNA, Anthony Trollope. Moving chronicle of Countess Lovel's bitter struggle to win for herself and daughter Anna their rightful rank and fortune—perhaps at cost of sanity itself. 384pp. 5⅜ × 8½. 24669-8 Pa. $6.95

EGYPTIAN MAGIC, E. A. Wallis Budge. Sums up all that is known about magic in Ancient Egypt: the role of magic in controlling the gods, powerful amulets that warded off evil spirits, scarabs of immortality, use of wax images, formulas and spells, the secret name, much more. 253pp. 5⅜ × 8½. 22681-6 Pa. $4.00

THE DANCE OF SIVA, Ananda Coomaraswamy. Preeminent authority unfolds the vast metaphysic of India: the revelation of her art, conception of the universe, social organization, etc. 27 reproductions of art masterpieces. 192pp. 5⅜ × 8½.
24817-8 Pa. $5.95

CATALOG OF DOVER BOOKS

CHRISTMAS CUSTOMS AND TRADITIONS, Clement A. Miles. Origin, evolution, significance of religious, secular practices. Caroling, gifts, yule logs, much more. Full, scholarly yet fascinating; non-sectarian. 400pp. 5⅜ × 8½.
23354-5 Pa. $6.50

THE HUMAN FIGURE IN MOTION, Eadweard Muybridge. More than 4,500 stopped-action photos, in action series, showing undraped men, women, children jumping, lying down, throwing, sitting, wrestling, carrying, etc. 390pp. 7⅞ × 10⅝.
20204-6 Cloth. $21.95

THE MAN WHO WAS THURSDAY, Gilbert Keith Chesterton. Witty, fast-paced novel about a club of anarchists in turn-of-the-century London. Brilliant social, religious, philosophical speculations. 128pp. 5⅜ × 8½.
25121-7 Pa. $3.95

A CEZANNE SKETCHBOOK: Figures, Portraits, Landscapes and Still Lifes, Paul Cezanne. Great artist experiments with tonal effects, light, mass, other qualities in over 100 drawings. A revealing view of developing master painter, precursor of Cubism. 102 black-and-white illustrations. 144pp. 8¾ × 6⅜.
24790-2 Pa. $5.95

AN ENCYCLOPEDIA OF BATTLES: Accounts of Over 1,560 Battles from 1479 B.C. to the Present, David Eggenberger. Presents essential details of every major battle in recorded history, from the first battle of Megiddo in 1479 B.C. to Grenada in 1984. List of Battle Maps. New Appendix covering the years 1967–1984. Index. 99 illustrations. 544pp. 6½ × 9¼.
24913-1 Pa. $14.95

AN ETYMOLOGICAL DICTIONARY OF MODERN ENGLISH, Ernest Weekley. Richest, fullest work, by foremost British lexicographer. Detailed word histories. Inexhaustible. Total of 856pp. 6½ × 9¼.
21873-2, 21874-0 Pa., Two-vol. set $17.00

WEBSTER'S AMERICAN MILITARY BIOGRAPHIES, edited by Robert McHenry. Over 1,000 figures who shaped 3 centuries of American military history. Detailed biographies of Nathan Hale, Douglas MacArthur, Mary Hallaren, others. Chronologies of engagements, more. Introduction. Addenda. 1,033 entries in alphabetical order. xi + 548pp. 6½ × 9¼. (Available in U.S. only)
24758-9 Pa. $11.95

LIFE IN ANCIENT EGYPT, Adolf Erman. Detailed older account, with much not in more recent books: domestic life, religion, magic, medicine, commerce, and whatever else needed for complete picture. Many illustrations. 597pp. 5⅜ × 8½.
22632-8 Pa. $8.50

HISTORIC COSTUME IN PICTURES, Braun & Schneider. Over 1,450 costumed figures shown, covering a wide variety of peoples: kings, emperors, nobles, priests, servants, soldiers, scholars, townsfolk, peasants, merchants, courtiers, cavaliers, and more. 256pp. 8⅜ × 11¼.
23150-X Pa. $7.95

THE NOTEBOOKS OF LEONARDO DA VINCI, edited by J. P. Richter. Extracts from manuscripts reveal great genius; on painting, sculpture, anatomy, sciences, geography, etc. Both Italian and English. 186 ms. pages reproduced, plus 500 additional drawings, including studies for *Last Supper*, *Sforza* monument, etc. 860pp. 7⅞ × 10¾. (Available in U.S. only) 22572-0, 22573-9 Pa., Two-vol. set $25.90

THE ART NOUVEAU STYLE BOOK OF ALPHONSE MUCHA: All 72 Plates from "Documents Decoratifs" in Original Color, Alphonse Mucha. Rare copyright-free design portfolio by high priest of Art Nouveau. Jewelry, wallpaper, stained glass, furniture, figure studies, plant and animal motifs, etc. Only complete one-volume edition. 80pp. 9⅜ × 12¼. 24044-4 Pa. $8.95

ANIMALS: 1,419 COPYRIGHT-FREE ILLUSTRATIONS OF MAMMALS, BIRDS, FISH, INSECTS, ETC., edited by Jim Harter. Clear wood engravings present, in extremely lifelike poses, over 1,000 species of animals. One of the most extensive pictorial sourcebooks of its kind. Captions. Index. 284pp. 9 × 12. 23766-4 Pa. $9.95

OBELISTS FLY HIGH, C. Daly King. Masterpiece of American detective fiction, long out of print, involves murder on a 1935 transcontinental flight—"a very thrilling story"—NY Times. Unabridged and unaltered republication of the edition published by William Collins Sons & Co. Ltd., London, 1935. 288pp. 5⅜ × 8½. (Available in U.S. only) 25036-9 Pa. $4.95

VICTORIAN AND EDWARDIAN FASHION: A Photographic Survey, Alison Gernsheim. First fashion history completely illustrated by contemporary photographs. Full text plus 235 photos, 1840-1914, in which many celebrities appear. 240pp. 6½ × 9¼. 24205-6 Pa. $6.00

THE ART OF THE FRENCH ILLUSTRATED BOOK, 1700-1914, Gordon N. Ray. Over 630 superb book illustrations by Fragonard, Delacroix, Daumier, Doré, Grandville, Manet, Mucha, Steinlen, Toulouse-Lautrec and many others. Preface. Introduction. 633 halftones. Indices of artists, authors & titles, binders and provenances. Appendices. Bibliography. 608pp. 8⅜ × 11¼. 25086-5 Pa. $24.95

THE WONDERFUL WIZARD OF OZ, L. Frank Baum. Facsimile in full color of America's finest children's classic. 143 illustrations by W. W. Denslow. 267pp. 5⅜ × 8½. 20691-2 Pa. $5.95

FRONTIERS OF MODERN PHYSICS: New Perspectives on Cosmology, Relativity, Black Holes and Extraterrestrial Intelligence, Tony Rothman, et al. For the intelligent layman. Subjects include: cosmological models of the universe; black holes; the neutrino; the search for extraterrestrial intelligence. Introduction. 46 black-and-white illustrations. 192pp. 5⅜ × 8½. 24587-X Pa. $6.95

THE FRIENDLY STARS, Martha Evans Martin & Donald Howard Menzel. Classic text marshalls the stars together in an engaging, non-technical survey, presenting them as sources of beauty in night sky. 23 illustrations. Foreword. 2 star charts. Index. 147pp. 5⅜ × 8½. 21099-5 Pa. $3.50

FADS AND FALLACIES IN THE NAME OF SCIENCE, Martin Gardner. Fair, witty appraisal of cranks, quacks, and quackeries of science and pseudoscience: hollow earth, Velikovsky, orgone energy, Dianetics, flying saucers, Bridey Murphy, food and medical fads, etc. Revised, expanded In the Name of Science. "A very able and even-tempered presentation."—The New Yorker. 363pp. 5⅜ × 8. 20394-8 Pa. $6.50

ANCIENT EGYPT: ITS CULTURE AND HISTORY, J. E Manchip White. From pre-dynastics through Ptolemies: society, history, political structure, religion, daily life, literature, cultural heritage. 48 plates. 217pp. 5⅜ × 8½. 22548-8 Pa. $4.95

SIR HARRY HOTSPUR OF HUMBLETHWAITE, Anthony Trollope. Incisive, unconventional psychological study of a conflict between a wealthy baronet, his idealistic daughter, and their scapegrace cousin. The 1870 novel in its first inexpensive edition in years. 250pp. 5⅜ × 8½. 24953-0 Pa. $5.95

LASERS AND HOLOGRAPHY, Winston E. Kock. Sound introduction to burgeoning field, expanded (1981) for second edition. Wave patterns, coherence, lasers, diffraction, zone plates, properties of holograms, recent advances. 84 illustrations. 160pp. 5⅜ × 8¼. (Except in United Kingdom) 24041-X Pa. $3.50

INTRODUCTION TO ARTIFICIAL INTELLIGENCE: SECOND, ENLARGED EDITION, Philip C. Jackson, Jr. Comprehensive survey of artificial intelligence—the study of how machines (computers) can be made to act intelligently. Includes introductory and advanced material. Extensive notes updating the main text. 132 black-and-white illustrations. 512pp. 5⅜ × 8½. 24864-X Pa. $8.95

HISTORY OF INDIAN AND INDONESIAN ART, Ananda K. Coomaraswamy. Over 400 illustrations illuminate classic study of Indian art from earliest Harappa finds to early 20th century. Provides philosophical, religious and social insights. 304pp. 6⅜ × 9⅜. 25005-9 Pa. $8.95

THE GOLEM, Gustav Meyrink. Most famous supernatural novel in modern European literature, set in Ghetto of Old Prague around 1890. Compelling story of mystical experiences, strange transformations, profound terror. 13 black-and-white illustrations. 224pp. 5⅜ × 8½. (Available in U.S. only) 25025-3 Pa. $5.95

ARMADALE, Wilkie Collins. Third great mystery novel by the author of *The Woman in White* and *The Moonstone*. Original magazine version with 40 illustrations. 597pp. 5⅜ × 8½. 23429-0 Pa. $9.95

PICTORIAL ENCYCLOPEDIA OF HISTORIC ARCHITECTURAL PLANS, DETAILS AND ELEMENTS: With 1,880 Line Drawings of Arches, Domes, Doorways, Facades, Gables, Windows, etc., John Theodore Haneman. Sourcebook of inspiration for architects, designers, others. Bibliography. Captions. 141pp. 9 × 12. 24605-1 Pa. $6.95

BENCHLEY LOST AND FOUND, Robert Benchley. Finest humor from early 30's, about pet peeves, child psychologists, post office and others. Mostly unavailable elsewhere. 73 illustrations by Peter Arno and others. 183pp. 5⅜ × 8½. 22410-4 Pa. $3.95

ERTÉ GRAPHICS, Erté. Collection of striking color graphics: *Seasons, Alphabet, Numerals, Aces* and *Precious Stones*. 50 plates, including 4 on covers. 48pp. 9⅜ × 12¼. 23580-7 Pa. $6.95

THE JOURNAL OF HENRY D. THOREAU, edited by Bradford Torrey, F. H. Allen. Complete reprinting of 14 volumes, 1837-61, over two million words; the sourcebooks for *Walden*, etc. Definitive. All original sketches, plus 75 photographs. 1,804pp. 8½ × 12¼. 20312-3, 20313-1 Cloth., Two-vol. set $80.00

CASTLES: THEIR CONSTRUCTION AND HISTORY, Sidney Toy. Traces castle development from ancient roots. Nearly 200 photographs and drawings illustrate moats, keeps, baileys, many other features. Caernarvon, Dover Castles, Hadrian's Wall, Tower of London, dozens more. 256pp. 5⅜ × 8¼. 24898-4 Pa. $5.95

AMERICAN CLIPPER SHIPS: 1833–1858, Octavius T. Howe & Frederick C. Matthews. Fully-illustrated, encyclopedic review of 352 clipper ships from the period of America's greatest maritime supremacy. Introduction. 109 halftones. 5 black-and-white line illustrations. Index. Total of 928pp. 5⅜ × 8½.
25115-2, 25116-0 Pa., Two-vol. set $17.90

TOWARDS A NEW ARCHITECTURE, Le Corbusier. Pioneering manifesto by great architect, near legendary founder of "International School." Technical and aesthetic theories, views on industry, economics, relation of form to function, "mass-production spirit," much more. Profusely illustrated. Unabridged translation of 13th French edition. Introduction by Frederick Etchells. 320pp. 6⅛ × 9¼. (Available in U.S. only) 25023-7 Pa. $8.95

THE BOOK OF KELLS, edited by Blanche Cirker. Inexpensive collection of 32 full-color, full-page plates from the greatest illuminated manuscript of the Middle Ages, painstakingly reproduced from rare facsimile edition. Publisher's Note. Captions. 32pp. 9⅜ × 12¼. 24345-1 Pa. $4.95

BEST SCIENCE FICTION STORIES OF H. G. WELLS, H. G. Wells. Full novel *The Invisible Man,* plus 17 short stories: "The Crystal Egg," "Aepyornis Island," "The Strange Orchid," etc. 303pp. 5⅜ × 8½. (Available in U.S. only)
21531-8 Pa. $4.95

AMERICAN SAILING SHIPS: Their Plans and History, Charles G. Davis. Photos, construction details of schooners, frigates, clippers, other sailcraft of 18th to early 20th centuries—plus entertaining discourse on design, rigging, nautical lore, much more. 137 black-and-white illustrations. 240pp. 6⅛ × 9¼.
24658-2 Pa. $5.95

ENTERTAINING MATHEMATICAL PUZZLES, Martin Gardner. Selection of author's favorite conundrums involving arithmetic, money, speed, etc., with lively commentary. Complete solutions. 112pp. 5⅜ × 8½. 25211-6 Pa. $2.95

THE WILL TO BELIEVE, HUMAN IMMORTALITY, William James. Two books bound together. Effect of irrational on logical, and arguments for human immortality. 402pp. 5⅜ × 8½. 20291-7 Pa. $7.50

THE HAUNTED MONASTERY and THE CHINESE MAZE MURDERS, Robert Van Gulik. 2 full novels by Van Gulik continue adventures of Judge Dee and his companions. An evil Taoist monastery, seemingly supernatural events; overgrown topiary maze that hides strange crimes. Set in 7th-century China. 27 illustrations. 328pp. 5⅜ × 8½. 23502-5 Pa. $5.95

CELEBRATED CASES OF JUDGE DEE (DEE GOONG AN), translated by Robert Van Gulik. Authentic 18th-century Chinese detective novel; Dee and associates solve three interlocked cases. Led to Van Gulik's own stories with same characters. Extensive introduction. 9 illustrations. 237pp. 5⅜ × 8½.
23337-5 Pa. $4.95

Prices subject to change without notice.

Available at your book dealer or write for free catalog to Dept. GI, Dover Publications, Inc., 31 East 2nd St., Mineola, N.Y. 11501. Dover publishes more than 175 books each year on science, elementary and advanced mathematics, biology, music, art, literary history, social sciences and other areas.